Enjoy Fans!

Hand Fans: An Illustrated History

A Timeline of Events, Materials, Arts and Technologies That Have Influenced Fans

Kathryn Finnegan

ISBN:9781519438294

INTRODUCTION

This is a chronology of hand fans which, from earliest times to the present day, have always been a creative expression of the time, place and unique cultures that produce them. This timeline follows the trail of their evolution and provides a look at the following:

How the most ordinary found objects evolved into highly sophisticated and ornamented ones, becoming symbols of authority and privilege, imbued with ceremonial - and for some - even mystical significance.

How artifacts such as carvings, pottery, murals and paintings, bear witness to the early use of fans where the written record is scant or non-existent.

How the invention of early forms of paper would eventually lead to fans covered with calligraphy, paintings and printing.

How the development of sericulture in B.C. China made possible the beautiful painted and embroidered fans of early China and centuries later, the elaborately decorated silk fans of Europe.

How the secrets of silk and papermaking were stolen and spread abroad.

How the word *fan* came into the English language – and how this word includes objects most would not even consider fans.

How fans were used by the early Christian church.

How Crusaders returning to England and Europe brought back refinements common to the Arab-controlled lands they travelled through, e.g., the all-but-forgotten fan.

How the powerful guilds of Europe that arose during the Middle Ages affected all phases of fan production till the end of the 18thC.

How the Protestant Reformation of the 16thC indirectly affected fan production in the 17thC and beyond.

How the Age of Western Exploration re-started trade with the Far East and brought folding fans to Europe.

How China produced very different fans for its trade with the West than those it made for home use.

How decoration on late 17th and 18thC European fans reflected the *chinoiserie* craze resulting from contact with the East, especially China.

How refinements in treating, decorating and scenting animal hides would make possible decoupé and painted fans made of vellum, parchment and other fine skins from the 17thC onward.

How various arts, e.g., the carving of ivory, mother-of-pearl and tortoiseshell, developed over many centuries in widespread geographic areas, found full expression in the beautiful fans of the 18th and 19th centuries.

How royalty in Europe and England popularized the use of fans and established fan etiquette.

How fans in the Far East (and initially in Europe) were enjoyed equally by men and women.

How fans in Europe went from being expensive novelties used to show off wealth and prestige to becoming common accessories available to the middle classes.

How the gradual development of different forms of printing led to the mass production of printed fans.

How printed fans functioned as an early form of mass media.

How technological developments changed social interactions and the uses of the fan.

How, inevitably, "fans followed fashion" – in style, size, materials and subject matter.

How every important movement/period in Western art played a role in fan decoration.

How wars and political events affected fan production and the dispersion of fans.

How early advertising made good use of fans.

How *Japonisme* (like the earlier fascination with China) not only captured the imagination of the public in the West, but caused Impressionist artists to re-think color, pattern and space and challenged them to fit paintings to the fan's curved format.

How roughly a century of World's Fairs, beginning in 1851, were a boon to the fan.

How a "Language of the Fan" came into the popular imagination.

How the 19thC became a century of invention, re-invention and hundreds of patents for fans.

How and why fan use declined rapidly in the West.

How, even if the artisans of yesteryear could be brought back, late 20th and 21stC sentiments about the treatment of animals would prevent them from re-creating their glorious creations.

How the fan, one of the oldest utilitarian/ceremonial objects invented by man, is still in use and vitally important in disparate cultures and geographic areas.

How interest in fans is being kept alive where fan use is no longer common.

Wishing you the pleasure of fans, whether encountering them for the first time – or revisiting old friends,

Kathryn Finnegan

GLOSSARY OF FAN TYPES

THERE ARE TWO BASIC FAN TYPES: FOLDING AND FIXED.

The two primary types of folding fans are **pleated** and **brisé. Cockades,** a third form, may be either pleated or brisé.

1. FOLDING FANS WITH A PLEATED LEAF:

Folding fans open to varying degrees from about 90 degrees to 180 degrees. The pleated fan may have a single or double leaf.

If the fan's leaf is opaque or double, the sticks are unseen from the front.

If sheer, the sticks show through.

FAN LEAF SIZES VARY:

very small

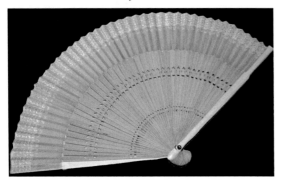

average

large

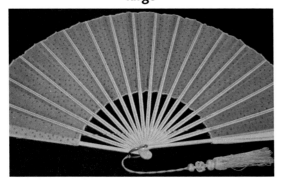

PARTS OF A PLEATED FAN:

Leaf: the pleated portion at the top of the fan, usually made of silk, paper or animal skins.

Ribs: sticks supporting the leaf.

Blades: sticks below the leaf which are often wider than the ribs behind the leaf.

Shoulder: blade area just below the leaf.

Guards: sturdy outermost sticks that protect the fan when closed. These are frequently ornamented so that even when closed, the fan has interest.

Gorge: area on fan immediately above the head.

Rivet: holds the sticks together, while allowing fan to open and close.

Head: area at bottom of fan, comprising the rivet and, if present, the washer and loop.

FRONT OF PLEATED FAN

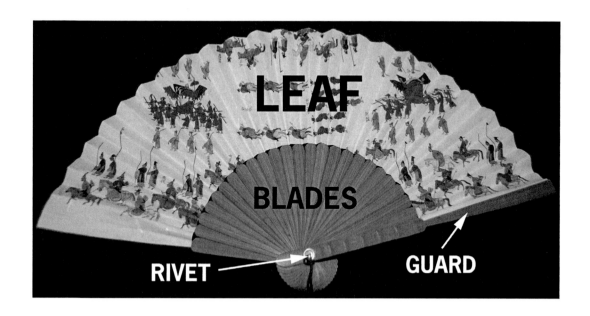

REVERSE OF PLEATED FAN

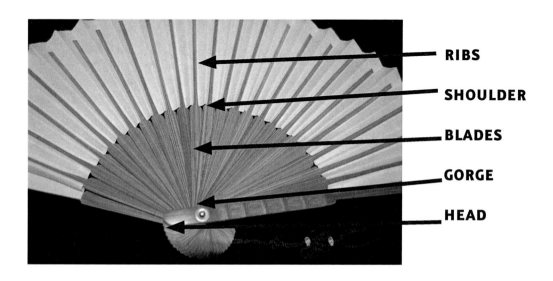

2. BRISÉ FANS:

These fans fold but instead of a pleated leaf, have separate segments called blades held together at the bottom by a rivet and near the top by a ribbon or thread.

Wooden Brisé

Palmette brisé fans,
a variation, have blades in leaf, petal or feather shapes. The blades are held in place by inconspicuously placed threads.

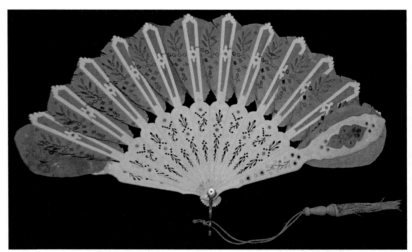
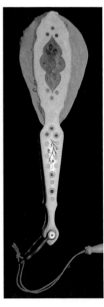

Bone and silk Palmette Brisé
with the sticks (unusually) placed in front of the silk "petals."

3. COCKADE FANS: Usually pleated, but may be brisés. These open around a central pivot– usually to 360 degrees.

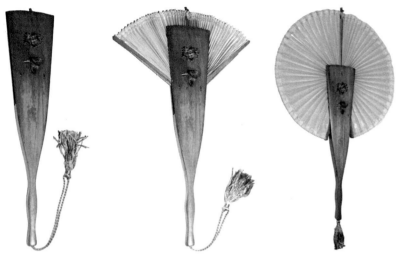

Cord at top of fan is pulled to open fan to 360 degrees. Bottom cord retracts the fan.

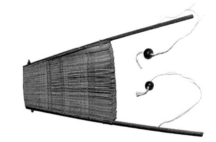

A Novelty Cockade

Double Cockade of split Palm leaf.

THE SECOND BASIC FAN TYPE IS THE FIXED (OR SCREEN) FAN WHICH DOES NOT FOLD:

1. Fixed fans with a distinct handle attached separately.

There are many variations of the attached handle *Fixed Fan*.

Embroidered silk stretched taut over a wooden frame.

Feathers supported by a thin metal frame with quills inserted into wooden handle.

Variations with wooden and bent reed handles:

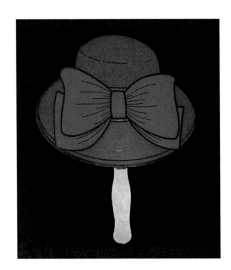

2. Fixed fans with "self-handles"

Fan made from a single stalk of Bamboo, split down to a node.

The top is cut into many splints which form the support for the paper leaf. This type is common in Japan and other Asian countries.

Frame of split Bamboo with silk leaf and a wooden-reinforced self-handle.

Palm Leaf Fans: one with Palm leaf stretched around a frame; one with a woven leaf. These are common throughout the islands of the South Pacific.

Unusual self-handle fan whittled from a single piece of wood.

Self-Handle Fans seen in the early – mid-20thC, were handed out for advertising and promotions or sold as souvenirs. Along with woven *Palm Leaf Fans*, these were commonly provided in churches, funeral parlors and other gathering places lacking air conditioning.

FANS CUT FROM A SINGLE PIECE OF CARDBOARD:

Comfy Hold Fan

Thumb Hold Fan

Tri-Fold Fan

Technically a *Folding Fan*, this *Self-handle Fan* is made of 3 pieces of cardboard held together with grommets. When "wings" on either side of the central panel are pulled, the fan opens to reveal the full scene.

A Timeline of Events, Materials, Arts And Technologies That Have Influenced Fans

B.C.

The first fans – a light-hearted speculation: After eviction from their garden paradise, Adam finds another use for the fig leaf and Eve picks up several feathers. They soon discover these found objects are useful for moving and cooling the air and for making cooking fires grow hotter, thus solving two post-Eden problems.

More conjecture: the next stage in fan making was to take found items and fashion them for specific uses, an advance over picking up leaves and feathers for moving the air. One of the earliest of these was the *Fly Whisk*, made from the tails of animals or threads of plant material attached to wood or bone handles. Another early type was a *Fixed Fan*, made of bark and other stiff materials, bound onto handles with grasses. From these strictly utilitarian objects, it was just a matter of time till fans were made with more attractive materials and decorated as they took on a third function - ceremonial use.

Egypt:
3,200-3,000 B.C.

From the *Proto-dynastic* period, a ritual artifact, probably a mace head, belonging to *King Scorpion II* and carved with several fans, is discovered. This may be the first documented use of the fan as a ceremonial object.

China:
2640 B.C.

Sericulture is invented when *Empress Su-Ling-she*, wife of *Emperor Hwang-te*, encouraged the cultivation of the Mulberry Tree, the rearing of worms and the reeling of silk.

2696 B.C.

The process of making cloth from silk is invented by *Leizu*, wife of *The Yellow Emperor*.

17thC B.C. - 1600-1100 B.C. (Shang Dynasty)

There are two written references to fans being used in ceremonies: one mentions a carriage bearing a fan and canopy of feathers; the other tells of 8 concubines carrying long-handled fans in a funeral procession for the Empress. At that time, large parasols were fixed on top of carriages to provide shade and protection from the elements. The parasols also functioned as fans, rotating with the airflow of the moving carriage. Tradition credits these large *Sunshade Fans* with providing the idea for later small, handheld fans. There is a long, historical association between parasols and fans, particularly in ceremonies and processions.

Egypt:
1543-1292 B.C. (18th Dynasty)

Fans belonging to *King Tutankhamen* (1334-1325 B.C.) were found in his tomb. Howard Carter who opened the tomb in 1922 describes them:

> *Upon a golden fan; found between the sepulchral shrines that covered and protected his sarcophagus, a fan, such as we see pictured in Roman times, and actually used today in the Vatican, is a beautifully embossed and chased picture of Tutankhamen, hunting ostriches for the plumes for that very flabellum. The second fan, larger and perhaps more resplendent, was of ebony, overlaid with sheet-gold and encrusted with turquoise, lapis lazuli, and carnelian-colored glass, as well as translucent calcite: the palm of the fan being emblazoned with the titulary of Tutankhamen.*

Unfortunately, only debris remained of the actual feathers but enough was left to show they had once been alternating brown and white Ostrich plumes, with forty-two on each fan. On the reverse of the golden fan, *Tutankhamen* is seen returning home from a successful hunt with the coveted feathers under his arm and with his attendants carrying two dead Ostriches.

Feather Fans may be regarded as the "Queen of Fans," due to their intrinsic beauty, frequent use in ceremonies and continuous use in geographically distant societies throughout recorded history.

Relics of lace (a network of knotted squares) and mummy cloths decorated with drawn work were found in tombs and catacombs in ancient Egypt. From earliest times, lace and fans have existed together, often leading parallel lives.

Egyptians make papyrus, an early paper, from a wetland Sedge that grew abundantly along the Nile Delta, but would not allow their writing material to be exported.

1279-1213 B.C. (19th Dynasty)

A bas relief shows *Ramses II (Ramses the Great)* accompanied by fan bearers with *Pole Fans*. The office of fan bearer was a favored position often held by the pharaoh's own sons.

Hand held fans and fans on poles are obviously related, a distinction being that the very long-handled fans must be wielded by a servant. *Pole Fan*s denote privilege and status and are associated with royalty, priestly functions or those wealthy enough to have servants to fan them.

Turkey:
c. 1,500 B.C.

Residents of Pergamum developed parchment from sheep skin, a writing material to rival Egypt's papyrus.

Israel:
8th – 7thC B.C.

The modern English word *Fan* comes from the Latin *Vannus,* an instrument for winnowing grain. These strictly agrarian "fans" are mentioned eight times in The Bible in the Old Testament books of the prophets *Isaiah, Jeremiah* and *Micah. Winnowing Fans* were made of heavy plaited straw, shaped like a scoop, often with handles attached to each side. When wheat, corn or millet had been cut and threshed, the grain still had to be separated from the husks. The farmer put down a wide mat and using his *Winnowing Fan* as a scoop, threw the grain into the air where the wind blew away the light chaff, while the heavier grains dropped onto the mat. There are frequent references in the Bible to "separating the wheat from the chaff."

China:

Woven Bamboo *Flag Fans* dating to 770-446 B.C., the earliest found, were unearthed in the *Liuzhou'ao* tomb in Jiangxi. Similar *Flag Fans* will be found in tomb sites in Hubei dating from the 5thC B.C. and in the Hunan Province dating from the 2ndC B.C.

The *Flag Fan*, one of the oldest and most enduring types, has either a stiff or flexible leaf mounted on one side of a thin handle and, like its name, resembles a flag on a pole.

Middle East:
7thC B.C.

Shell carving has evolved as a specialized art. Many centuries later, the highly sophisticated carving of mother-of-pearl, tortoiseshell, etc. will add great beauty to fans.

Assyria:
7thC B.C.

A bas relief shows an attendant in a procession holding *Fly Whisks*.

China:
7thC B.C. (or earlier)

The *Tuan Shan*, a round *Screen Fan* made of silk appears and will remain the preferred type in China for many centuries. Its shape, like a full moon, carries the auspicious meanings of union and happiness.

Greece:
5th - 4th centuries B.C.

The center of civilization shifts from Egypt to Greece. Early Greek fans were made of Myrtle and Acacia woods. Then fans made of papyrus, based on Egyptian design appeared, probably through trade with the Phoenicians. Circular *Peacock Feather Fans* were also in use. Works of art show wealthy Greeks being fanned by slaves waving *Pole Fans* with screens in the shape of Palmetto leaves. Personal hand held *Screen Fans* were also used; a surviving example is housed in the *Staatliche Museum* in Berlin. A statue from this period shows a woman holding a heart-shaped fan.

China:
4thC B.C.

Paper, probably made from raw silk cocoons and known as silk paper was in use.

Mesopotamia:
3rdC B.C.

In Ur, mother-of-pearl was used decoratively. Carving in relief, inlay, mosaic work, engraving and even a form of shell intarsia or marquetry were all employed.

China
250 B.C.

Calligraphy, more highly esteemed than painting as an art, is advanced when scholar, *Meng T'ien*, invents the camel hair brush to draw characters, work previously done with clumsy pointed sticks.

210 B.C.

Lacquering of articles as a protective and decorative coating was done hundreds of years B.C. (no exact date known). The Chinese maintained their supremacy in this art till the 17thC when they were surpassed by the Japanese.

206 B.C. – 220 A.D.

China's first Emperor, *Qin Shi Huang*, enlarges various earlier fortifications into what became known as *The Great Wall*. At the same time that China was protecting its borders, it established an extensive trade route to the West. Known as *The Silk Road*, it encompassed both land and sea routes. This emperor is remembered today for the terra cotta warriors protecting his tomb in Xi'an.

2ndC B.C.
Roman Empire:

Spices, silk and other goods from as far away as China, now reach the Roman Empire via *The Silk Road*. Silver flows out of Rome in exchange for highly prized commodities from the Far East.

1stC B.C.
China:

The round *Screen Fan* is documented in murals and texts. Fans were generally discarded in the autumn so a lady whose charms have faded or a deserted lover was referred to as an *Autumn Fan*.

This is a translation of the poem, *A Song of Resentment*, attributed to *Lady Ban*, a royal concubine, who suffered this very fate:

> *Thin white silk, newly cut and trimmed,*
> *Fresh and pure as frost or snow.*
> *Made into a fan for joyous meetings,*
> *Perfectly round like the brilliant moon.*
> *It goes in and out of my Master's sleeve,*
> *Waves back and forth, makes a gentle breeze.*
> *But I often fear the arrival of autumn,*
> *With cold gales which drive out the burning heat.*
> *Then it's tossed aside into a wicker basket,*
> *Affection cut off midway.*

A.D. 1st – 2nd centuries

1stC

Antiquity and the Roman Empire

The word *fan* (the agrarian winnowing instrument) is found again in the New Testament books of *Matthew, Luke* and *Revelation* which date to this century. Romans had 3 words for their distinctive types of fans: the *Vannus* for winnowing grain, the *Muscarium* or *Fly Whisk* and the *Flabellum* for moving air. Slaves waved *Flabella* similar to those of the pharaohs, with handles up to six feet high, topped with semi-circles of feathers. Peacock feathers were particularly popular both in Greece and Rome.

Earlier Etruscans were highly skilled metal smiths and great care was taken in the production of the fan's handles. Less wealthy Romans had bunches of feathers bound to short handles of wood or metal.

37-68

A Roman, *Carvilius Pollio*, used tortoiseshell plates to veneer furniture, the earliest recorded use of this art. Even earlier, the Greeks may have been using whole shells for their lyres. Tortoiseshell would eventually become a prized material for fan blades and guards.

2ndC

Antiquity and the Roman Empire:

The *Flabellum* was a fan used in the early Roman Christian church and for many centuries thereafter. Two deacons at either end of the altar waved *Flabella* to prevent insects from landing on the chalice or host. There were two types of *Flabella* (both round): the cockade and the disc, both usually decorated. The disc was made of metal, leather or Peacock feathers. The cockade was a pleated round of parchment or other fine skin. When closed the cockade leaf folded into a thin rectangular box for protection. In the Greek Orthodox church, the *Flabellum* was called a *Ripidion*.

Another early ecclesiastical fan was the *Muscarium*, a *Fly Whisk* made of animal hairs to sweep away insects.

2nd – 4th centuries

The *Carlisle Museum* in England has a canopied tombstone with a carving of a lady holding an open *Cockade Fan*. It dates from the 2nd-3rd centuries and may be the earliest depiction of a Roman/British fan.

China:

Two fan types, the *Fly Whisk*, made of horse or deer tails and traditionally used by men as a symbol of rank and *Palm Leaf Fans* (often painted) appear in written records.

105

The eunuch, *Ts'ai Lun*, invented true paper. With this invention, the new brushed calligraphy characters became an art form.

By the end of the 2ndC, block printing was possible as the Chinese now had the three necessary elements: paper, ink and surfaces with texts carved in relief.

3rdC

The Roman Empire:
An engraved Roman goblet shows a slave holding a *Flag Fan*. The Roman *Flag Fan* consisted of a square or rectangle of cloth or skin attached to the side of a long, thin handle. They may have found their way to Rome from Egypt.

4thC

Cockade Fans, shown in a drawing, are still in use in Roman England. The Yorkshire Museum has a pair of ivory fan handles from a 4thC burial site.

Egypt:
Flag Fans from the Christian Coptic church of the 4th-6th centuries have been preserved. *Flag Fans*, one of the oldest types, are still made in Egypt and other African countries.

China:
The first fan with calligraphy is thought to be a fan with the handwriting of *Wang Xizhi* (302-362), traditionally referred to as the *Sage of Calligraphy*.

Japan: 300
The Japanese secured the secret of silk manufacture by abducting four Chinese girls who revealed the process. Thus began the Japanese silk industry.

6thC

Europe:
The fan, like so many refinements of the Roman Empire, largely vanished from the scene in England and Europe, not to be revived till centuries later as these areas reacquired a veneer of civilization, thanks in no small measure to trade with the Arab world and the Far East.

China:
Wood block printing is in use.

Japan:

Representations of fans (ovals with stripes on long poles) are found in a burial mound on the island of Kyushu and are perhaps the earliest examples of fans in Japanese art.

7thC

Italy:

A folding cockade *Flabellum* intended for secular use and said to have belonged to the Lombard Queen, *Theolinda*, resides in the *Basilica of St. John the Baptist* in Monza. The date is disputed, but it is a rare example of a *Flabellum* made for non-ecclesiastical use.

Yucatan Peninsula:

In what today is southern Mexico, Guatemala and Belize, paintings, pottery and monuments show *Mayan* fans from the 7th-9th centuries. Types include the *Fly Whisk, Parasol, Shield, Flag* and *Feather Fans*, as well as round and variously shaped *Plaited* and *Woven Fans*.

China:

In the time of *Emperor Kao-tsong* (650-653) an account is given of fans made of Pheasant feathers with long ivory handles, carried on either side of the Emperor. A handscroll from this period shows a court lady with a round *Pole Fan*.

Japan: 615

Paper is introduced to Japan. *Sutras* (sacred texts) from Buddhism, a new religion from India, were copied by monks and the wide dissemination of *sutras* on paper scrolls facilitated the spread of Buddhism in Japan.

Silk, a staple of Japanese fan-making, was increasingly combined with paper to make a 50-50 mixture for added strength and durability. Fine silk cloth, silken tassels and cords were used to make *Uchiwa* (fixed *Screen Fans*).

Though the Chinese and Koreans contest its origin, the *Folding Fan* was probably invented in Japan in the 7thC. The first ones may have been brisés (*Hi-ogi*), made of 25 thin strips of wood, connected at the bottom by a rivet and at the top by a cord in such a way that they could be easily separated and then folded back together. They were probably modeled on *Mokkan*, early court tablets of threaded thin wooden or ivory leaves. These early court tablets, carried by officials to write on, were also in use in *pre-Han* China.

8thC

Spain:
Muslims invade Spain in 711 and are dominant there for the next 750 years. With the Moorish conquest, new techniques for working and decorating leather with gold and silver and treating leather with scents were introduced. Cordoba, the capital of Muslim Spain, was the center of this industry. From pre-Roman times Spain had been a country of traders. Now ships that docked in Seville brought treasures from areas under Muslim control in the Levant, including Iraq, Jerusalem and Crete, as well as central Asia, North Africa, Southern Italy, Sicily and Sardinia. Overland routes brought luxuries including woven textiles from China. The *Flag Fan* appears wherever there is Arab influence.

Persia:
Persia is the center of shell carving. This work flourished in the Arab states where Islamic geometrical and abstract designs were used.

Uzbekistan (modern day name): 750-751
Near Samarkand, a city that occupied a central position on *The Silk Road*, Chinese prisoners taken at the *Battle of Talas* gave the secret of papermaking to the Arabs and from that time, paper mills proliferated in Arab-controlled areas.

9thC

Spain:
At the end of the 9thC, the *Codice of Azagra* records the gift of a fan with raised gold letters given to *Lady Guisinda* from her husband, *Count Guifredo*.

China: 868
Wood block printing is first used to print an entire book, *The Diamond Sutra*.

Japan: 894
The *Heian* government suspended official relations with China and from the

end of the 9thC, the life of the court will be less influenced by Chinese art and culture which had permeated Japan from the 3rd to the 6th centuries.

10thC
MIDDLE AGES

Spain:
The cultivation of the silkworm is well established and Spain has its own textile industry and is known for the vast variety it produces. Imported paper is in use by 950.

Korea:
A particular type of *Screen Fan* is believed to have originated in Korea. It is made from a single piece of Bamboo, split down to a node to prevent further splitting. The intact section below the node forms the handle, while the wood above is cut into 50-60 thin splints and splayed out to provide a firm base. A leaf of silk or paper is then stretched and pasted onto either side.

Though disputed, Korean art historians also believe the *Folding Fan* was invented by a Buddhist monk during the *Goryeo Dynasty* (910-1392) and taken from Korea to Japan and from there to China.

China:
The *Tuan Shan*, the round silk *Screen Fan* (oval, square, rectangular with rounded corners, hexagon, octagon, gourd shape and other variations, but all considered "round") has been around for centuries. Now the *Tuan Shan* becomes something more as artists, including members of the court - even the Emperor – paint them and they become known as *Palace Fans*. Treasured as artwork, they were often dismounted from their frames and re-mounted as album leaves, a custom that preserved many of them.

960-1126 (late *Northern Song*)
Earliest examples of painting and calligraphy on fans date to this period.

According to a written reference, the Chinese initially ridiculed the Japanese *Folding Fan* which was favored only by courtesans who probably acquired them from Japanese sailors. It took about 500 years for *Folding Fans* to become respectable and accepted, until eventually they became the popular choice.

960-1278
China lost her possessions in Central Asia and entered an isolationist period, virtually severing connections with the West. A Japanese literary work dated 960 indicates the *Folding Fan* had reached China by that date, though they did not become popular there till centuries later. Their slow acceptance in China is another argument for their origin elsewhere. A handscroll shows female attendants with very large, rectangular *Pole Fans*.

Japan:
Most scholars believe the Japanese invented two types of *Folding Fans*. The first type has a number of blades joined together at the bottom with a rivet and at the top with a string or ribbon (*Hi-ogi*) The other type is a fan with sticks joined at the bottom with a rivet, with the top portion covered with a paper or silk pleated leaf (*Ogi*). A popular legend says the design of the *Ogi* was based on one man's careful observation of a bat's wings opening and closing. The earliest *Ogi* had 15 Bamboo sticks, a single leaf and an open arc of about 90 degrees.

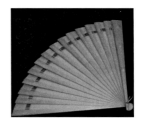 

The other popular style is the *Screen Fan* (*Uchiwa*). A dictionary compiled during the 930's lists both *Ogi* and *Uchiwa*. Over time the Japanese will develop dozens of types of *Ogi* and *Uchiwa* for specific uses - each with its own distinguishing name.

11thC
MIDDLE AGES

Europe:
As the century was ending (1095), *Pope Urban II* proclaimed the *First Crusade* with the stated purpose of restoring Christian access to holy places in and near Jerusalem. Crusades to areas under Muslim control continued sporadically over the next 200 years, resulting in trading with countries lying beyond the eastern borders of Europe. Crusaders returned with tales of life in exotic Middle Eastern cities and souvenirs, including, we may suppose, the fans commonly used in warm climates.

Guilds, the trade associations for crafts and industries, flourished from the 11thC. Guilds eventually controlled the various aspects of fan making and were to play a very important role in their production for the next 800 years.

China: 1041
Movable type for printing is invented by the alchemist, *Pi Sheng*.

Japan:
Two great literary works completed in the early 11thC, *Tale of Genji* by *Lady Murasaki Shikibu* and *Pillow Book* by *Lady Sei Shōnagon* give a picture of the decoration and function of fans in *Heian* court life.

The early *Screen Fan* (*Uchiwa*) loses in popularity to the *Pleated* "bat" *Fan* (*Ogi*) and the folding brisé (*Hi-ogi*). Block printing was sometimes used to decorate these fans.

12thC
MIDDLE AGES

Europe:
Paper arrived through the Italian ports that had active trade relations with the Arab world. The knowledge of papermaking made its way into Spain in 1151.

Italy:
Various types of fans likely reached Italy via crusaders returning from the Middle East. Warm, humid cities such as Venice, Genoa and Sienna, lying in the path of homebound Christians, were ideal for personal fans.

France:
Fans were present at the royal court. An illuminated manuscript shows *Louis VII* lying on his sick bed being fanned with a *Flag Fan*.

Cambodia:
12th – 13thC carved reliefs on temples, including those at Angkor Wat, show at least five different types of fans. Most are *Pole Fans* with handles about 3 feet in length. Carvings show the fans being used in processions, ceremonies and an elephant hunt.

China:
1127-1279 (*Southern Song*)
Written records indicate that *Folding Fans* were being made in Hangzhou where production continues today. Open, this early fan had a wedge shape. It was not as effective as the *Screen Fan* at creating a breeze and did not become popular till much later during the *Ming Dynasty*.

Japan:

Paintings make it clear that by the end of the 12thC, decorated paper *Folding Fans* were in widespread use and far outnumbered the few depictions of the *Screen Fan*.

13thC
MIDDLE AGES

Persia:

Persian miniatures from this period show *Flag Fans*.

Europe:

Flag Fans are seen in European paintings from the 13thC.

The fashion for decorating with sequins or *paillettes*, (the French embroidery term) appears. These were made by coiling a round silver wire tightly around a long core of wood or metal and then cutting the wire to release a series of small rings. Each wire ring was hammered flat to produce a round shiny sequin with a hole in the center so it could be sewn onto clothing and other items. Round sequins and variously shaped spangles would later become very fashionable as a decoration on European fans.

Italy:

Papermaking centers grew in Italy after 1275 and in France and Germany during the 14thC. In Western Europe the elements essential for printing were slowly coming together as a favorable trade, cultural and economic climate was emerging.

Marco Polo journeys to China and returns with such amazing tales of the opulent court of the *Mongol* empire that many dismiss his report as fantasy. The city of Venice becomes a main European port of entry and departure to and from the Orient, making the city very influential and rich from its trade with the East.

By 1283 a guild for painters and lacquerists exists in Venice.

China:
1260

Kubla Khan, a *Mongol*, ascends the throne of China as first Emperor of the *Yuan Dynasty*. The *Mongols* re-open the caravan routes, restoring communications between East and West. Chinese art, in all fields, flourishes during this period.

EARLY EUROPEAN RENAISSSANCE and CHINA'S MING DYNASTY
14thC

Europe:
Miniatures and engravings from this period show ladies with long-handled, round fans made of feathers or rice straw. The fan soon came to be an indispensable part of the ensemble of high born ladies and reflected the costliness of their dress. *Feather Fans* and *Flag Fans* were the preferred styles throughout Europe.

Fan motifs, indicative of the fan's popularity, appear on lacquerware, sword guards, ceramics, pottery, prints, textiles and family crests.

By this date the Roman Catholic church has largely discontinued the use of *Flabella* to chase insects from the host and chalice during the Mass. The exception was the use of very large feather *Flabella* on long handles carried in Papal processions which continued to be used till Vatican II in the 1960's.

Xylography or printing from a wood block which originated in China in the 9thC, appeared in Europe around the end of the 14th century.

Italy:
Three types of fans were popular: *Ostrich Fans*, *Flag Fans* and a *Fixed Fan* shaped in a quarter or half circle. *Ostrich Fans* made of feathers from North Africa, bleached or dyed and inserted into handles were preferred in upper and central Italy. A small fan with a long, thin handle and 5-7 plumes, set symmetrically, was favored by the ladies of Parma, Ferrara and Florence. Some *Feather Fans* resembled a feather duster; in another style, the feathers were laid flat. Portraits show an effort to make the feathers match the colors of ladies' gowns. Ladies of Venice and Padua also used these tuft *Feather Fans* but preferred *Flag Fans*, the simple ones made of woven straw, but the finest made of gold brocade, cut parchment, lace work or decorated and gilt leather. The handles of the best fans might be made of gold or silver embellished with precious stones.

France:

From inventories, the following fans of royalty are listed:

1316   the *Countess Mahaut* of Artois: a fan with a silver handle

1328   *Queen Clemence*, wife of *Louis X*: a fan of embroidered silk

1372   *Queen Johanna d'Evereux*, widow of *Louis X*: a fan made of gold cloth, decorated with coats of arms of France and Navarre with an ivory staff

1380   *Charles V*: a round *Ivory Fan* bearing the coats of arms of France and Navarre on an ebony staff; 3 banners (probably *Flag Fans*) made of carved leather with gilt silver staffs; 2 banners from France embroidered with lilies and pearls to *"fan the king when he sits at table."*

England:

The earliest records of the fan in Renaissance England date from 1307 in the inventory of *Isabella of France* who became Queen of England when she married *Edward II*.

During the reign of *Richard II* (1367-1400) fans were used by male and female royalty and members of the court.

China:

1368-1644 (*The Ming Dynasty*)

China passes once more into the hands of a Chinese ruling house and again becomes isolationist, closing her borders to Western "barbarians." At the very moment when Europe was poised to make great technological advances and become a world power, China turned inward, missing the opportunity.

First seen in the 10thC, *Palace Fans*, screens embroidered with floral designs or decorated with paintings or calligraphy, are still the preferred style, but increasingly share pride of place with *Folding Fans*.

The Chinese invent a paper-cutting technique which would later become known in Europe as *decoupé*. These lace-like perforations would become a popular decoration on fans beginning in the 16thC.

Japan:

1333-1568 (*The Muromachi Period*)

Fan painting becomes an established branch of art and leading artists produce paintings for fans. Many of these were never mounted; the challenge of creating a design appropriate to the fan's format was considered paramount. Ironically, this would be the same challenge taken up by Western *Impressionist* artists three centuries later.

There was renewed contact with China and Korea. Chinese fans were introduced to Japan. The most unusual feature of these to Japanese eyes was the use of a double leaf. Monochromatic paintings in the Chinese style were reproduced by Japanese artists who rapidly developed their own style.

15thC RENAISSANCE
THE AGE OF WESTERN EXPLORATION BEGINS

Portugal was first; Spain next.

1394-1460   *Henry "the Navigator"* of Portugal sets off the *Age of Discovery* by searching for a route East by South to China.

1488   *Bartholomew Diaz* of Portugal rounds the Cape of Good Hope, Africa. This trip is significant because Portugal realizes they can now trade with India and the East without taking the long overland route with its dangers and expensive middle men.

1492   With a growing rivalry between Portugal and Spain, *Christopher Columbus* is granted a subsidy by Spain's *King Ferdinand* and *Queen Isabella* to find a new route to the East, but discovers instead islands in the Caribbean. When *Columbus* returns from his first trip he presents *Queen Isabella* with a *Feather Fan* from the New World.

1494   Spain and Portugal sign a treaty giving Portugal claim to Africa, India and the Eastern portion of Brazil. Spain is given everything else in the New World.

1497	*Vasco da Gama*, another Portuguese explorer, makes the sea trip to India around the Cape of Good Hope. Over the next 20 years he makes three other journeys, extending as far as China and from there to Japan in 1517.
1498	The earliest Portuguese explorers reach Japan. Two years later, they were visiting regularly.

1430
Holland: Metallographic printing appears.

1450
Germany:
Though movable type was invented in China in 1041, it becomes available in Europe when *Gutenberg* invents a printing press.

Spain:
1492
The expulsion of Jews, Muslims and others not baptized as Catholics will bring the skills of these ostracized people to other areas.

Mexico:
Pre-Columbian Mexicans were highly skilled in the decorative use of feathers on fans. At first they used feathers from Heron and Duck, but by the time of *Montezuma*, the rarest tropical birds with flashing iridescent plumage were obtained by the Emperor's merchants from all parts of the *Aztec* empire. Golden-green feathers from the Quetzal, red-pink from the Spoonbill, brilliant plumes from the Parrot, Troupial, Crested Guan and Blue Cotinga were all used in intricate mosaic-like patterns, applied to *Fixed Fans*.

France:
The guild of *Tabletiers*, primarily makers of wooden tablets joined with the ivory and inlay craftsmen, becoming a single guild but retaining the name *Tabletiers*. Around 1440 the *Tabletiers* joined forces with the *Oigniers* (comb makers) and *Deciers* (makers of dice, tables, pawns, chess boards and other small items). Over time their repertoire expanded till eventually they gained the right to work with numerous exotic materials and to make a wide variety of objects, including fan sticks and guards.

China:

Carved Ivory Brisé Fans became fashionable. At first they were fretted and pierced with carving limited to the sticks, but as the Chinese perfected their carving and as ivory fans gained in popularity, the entire fan was intricately carved.

16thC — HIGH RENAISSANCE
THE AGE OF EXPLORATION CONTINUES

Portugal & Spain still dominate:

1502   The King of Portugal obtains from *Pope Alexander VI* a Papal Bull making him "*Lord of the Navigation, Conquests, and Trade of Ethiopia, Arabia, Persia and India.*"

1511   The Portuguese establish a base at Malacca.

1511   The Spice Islands and Java are discovered.

1516   Portuguese explorers are the first to reach China and establish a trading post at Ningpo.

1517   *Vasco da Gama* of Portugal reaches Japan.

1517   The King of Portugal sends a delegation to Canton to meet the Chinese Emperor. They are granted trading rights, but soon displeased their host and are expelled in 1522. Forty years later, they were allowed to establish a base at Macau.

1519   Spaniard, *Hernan Cortez*, lands on the coast of Mexico and proceeds to Tenochtitlan (present-day Mexico City) to meet with the *Aztec Emperor, Montezuma II*. As a symbol of his authority, *Montezuma* was accompanied by a circular *Fixed Fan* of brilliantly colored feathers held high on a wooden pole. *Cortez* sends fourteen *Feather Fans* back to Spain. 16thC Spanish records of *Inca* life in the Andes tell of warehouses full of fine textiles and featherwork. *Fly Whisks* and fans of brightly colored feathers were in use by the *Incans*.

1543   Defeat of the Portuguese by the Spanish opens the opportunity to other European nations to develop trade.

1549   The Portuguese Jesuit priest, *Francis Xavier*, established the first Christian mission in Japan. By the end of the century there were many converts, a development Japanese rulers viewed with alarm.

1557   The trading port of Macau in China is established by the Portuguese who maintained it till 1887.

Turkey:
Miniature paintings of life in Istanbul in 1582 show *Ottoman* figures carrying *Flag Fans*, evidence of their continued use in Islamic countries.

Europe:
The Protestant Reformation and resulting Catholic/Protestant schism resulted in wars, massacres and witch hunts. Art was moving through *Mannerism* into the *Baroque*. This was the age of *Caravaggio, Rembrandt, Rubens* and *Bernini*. Portraits were often painted to display newly acquired wealth and position or to commemorate important occasions. The abrupt appearance of *Folding Fans* in portraits in the late 16thC indicated something new and important in fashion.

Painted Fans came in just as the *High Renaissance* faded away. No great artists of the 16thC painted fans – or at least have been recorded doing so.

The century began with various types of *Feather Fans* being the most common and ended with the popularity of *Pleated Fans*. These were made of thick paper or leather and opened to a quarter circle. During the 16thC fans were common in courts all over Europe and by the end of the century were being exported from one country to another, having become desirable accessories for women outside the courts.

Lace:
From the 16thC on, lace played a significant role in European fan leaves. During this century lace became very important, both as fashion accessory and as an industry in Venice, France and Spain. Lace making was a laborious and time consuming process which made it expensive. Initially used for ecclesiastical purposes such as altar cloths and alb flounces, soon royalty and aristocracy were using large pieces of lace for collars, ruffs and cuffs. Men adorned their shoes with lace rosettes and cuffs hanging from their boots.

Starching was introduced into England in 1564 and this, together with prods and irons helped to promote the fashion of enormous ruffs where some means of fixing the lace was required. The earliest *Lace Fans* date from the mid-16thC and were composed of lace inserted into parchment or taffeta backgrounds.

Starching and re-pleating a fan would not be practical, so it is possible that *Decoupé Fans* of paper and vellum were created to simulate the look of lace. *Eleanor of Austria* who married both *King Manuel I* of Portugal and later *King Francis I* of France was influential in popularizing lace fashions.

In the 16thC, 156 pattern books for embroidery and lace were printed, mainly in Germany and Venice, though one of the most important lace pattern books was published in Paris in 1587 by *Federic de Vinciolo*. In the 16th – 18th centuries laces were named after the towns in which they were made, but by the 19thC, these were merely types of laces and might be made anywhere.

Lace would wax and wane in popularity over the next three centuries, reaching its last great popularity in the final quarter of the 19thC.

Iberian Peninsula:

Because Portugal had special Papal concessions allowing them to trade with China, the *Folding Fan* was probably introduced first to Portugal and soon after to Spain. The *Prado Museum* in Madrid has a portrait by *Cuello*, c.1570, showing a lady holding a closed *Pleated Fan*, one of the earliest examples of this new type of fan in European art.

In Spain, pleated *Lace Fans* went hand-in-hand with the pleated lace ruffs then in vogue. Spanish *Catherine of Aragon* (*Henry VIII's* first wife) was instrumental in promoting the latest fashions made of lace and introduced lace making into Buckinghamshire, England.

Mexico:

In 1519, Spanish explorer, *Hernan Cortes*, landed on the coast of Mexico near what would become the port of Veracruz. He was met by ambassadors of the *Aztec Emperor, Montezuma*, and was given many gifts, including fans. Among the treasures sent back to Spain, 14 fans of colored featherwork, some embellished with gold, are listed. Early manuscripts describe three basic types of *Feather Fans*: round, half circle and feathers mounted upright on a handle. *Aztec* costume and accessory was regulated by strict laws and indicated a person's rank and status. Fans were also used in their dances, healing rituals and other ceremonies. *Aztec* featherworkers, both men and women, were highly skilled artisans who "painted with feathers." The feathers were applied either with glue or bound in place with thread from the Maguey plant in elaborate mosaic-like patterns. The work was so highly regarded that it was performed by nobles as well as the artisans. This was one of the few native arts that impressed the Spanish enough to encourage feather artisans to produce items for export following the fall of Tenochtitlan.

Among the fans that *Cortes* sent back to his king, *Charles V*, one now known as the *Ambras Fan*, survives today in Hofburg, Vienna in the *Museum fur Volkekunde*. It is a ceremonial fan on a long handle. The body consists of threads interwoven in concentric rings on a wooden frame. The rings are covered with leather and Agave paper to which a mosaic of primary-colored feathers is glued. The fringe is made of feathers from the Quetzal (*Pharomacrus moccinno*), a rare Central American bird.

The Andes:
Fans have existed in the Andes for at least 2,000 years as a status symbol and as a connection to the mystic world. Spanish explorers were astonished to find *Inca* warehouses filled with fine textiles instead of gold. One fan was described as having bright Parrot and Hummingbird feathers radiating out from a cane handle.

Italy:
Paintings show women holding long-handled *Feather Duster Fans* and *Flag Fans* made of plaited straw, embroidered fabrics and incised leather. Venice was especially noted for its *Ventoli* (*Flag Fans*). Engravings intended for *Ventoli* were double images, printed on one sheet, folded over and stuck onto the handle.

The first true *Folding Fans* appeared in Italy around the middle of the 16thC and were probably part of the Venetian trade with the Orient. One of the earliest, used by the ladies of Ferrara, was the *Duck Foot Fan*, so named because when fully opened to a quarter circle, it resembled the webs between a duck's toes. It was mounted on 8 very narrow ivory sticks. The leaves were formed of strips of vellum, inset with mica, delicately painted and topped with ball finials.

Another early style of *Folding Fan* was the *Decoupé*. These were made of vellum or thick paper, finely cut to resemble reticella lace.

The *Commedia dell'Arte* developed in the regions of the Veneto and Lombardy in the 16thC and was brought to the court of France by *Catherine de Medici*. Its beloved comic figures, *Harlequin*, *Pierrot*, *Pierrette* and other stock characters would become the subject on many fans. *Pierrot*-themed fans were especially popular in the late 19th and early 20th centuries.

France:
Dieppe has become a major center for the carving of ivory and will remain so for centuries.

Catherine de Medici, a niece of *Pope Leo X* who granted Papal trading concessions to Portugal, would have been familiar with the newest novelties coming from the East, including fans. When she married *King Henri II* of France in 1533, she brought various refinements from Italy to the French court. In addition to bringing with her the *Commedia dell'Arte*, her cooks introduced the French to peas, beans, spinach and olive oil. She also brought perfume and her fans. She is said to have introduced the French to *Feather Fans*, worn at the waist and attached to a gold chain, a fashion already in general use in Italy. She also brought the very new, round *Screen Fans*.

Henri III, son of *Catherine de Medici*, used fans as did other men in his court. They were probably used less for cooling and more as a showy and novel accessory. An account from 1588 says he held in his right hand a *decoupé* vellum *Folding Fan* with a lace border, large enough to serve as both fan and parasol. His wife is shown in a tapestry holding a *Feather Fan* with a jeweled holder in a handle about 10 inches long. In an engraving, she is also seen carrying a *Duck Foot Fan*.

England:
During the reign of *Henry VIII* (1491-1547) *Feather Fans* were carried by gentlemen as well as ladies. Not a great deal is recorded of this period, but the essayist, *George Steevens* writes:

Even young gentlemen carried fans of feathers in their hands,
which in war our ancestors wore on their heads.

In 1556 *Queen Mary*, daughter of *Henry VIII*, received:
 Seven fannes to kepe the heate of the fyre, of straw, the one of white silk.
This is an early reference to the use of *Fire Screens* designed to protect
the complexion (or to prevent the melting of heavy makeup as a result
of sitting too near a fire). On inventory lists, personal fans were listed
separately from *Fire Screens* which were viewed more as an accessory for
the home.

Queen Elizabeth I (1533-1603) was a great lover of fans. She considered
a fan the most suitable present a sovereign could receive from her
subjects and was given fans by *Sir Francis Drake* and another of her
favorites, *Robert Dudley*, Earl of Leicester. *Elizabeth* was proud of her
lovely hands and was often painted holding a fan – usually feathers,
but later in her reign, the newer *Folding Fans*. At her death in 1603, she
owned 27 fans which are described in her wardrobe lists.

17th C
THE AGE OF WESTERN EXPLORATION CONTINUES –
WITH NEW PLAYERS

1600   The English found the *East India Company* (also operating in
        Amoy and Canton, China).

1602   The Dutch establish the *Vereenigde Ost-Indische Compagnie.*

1603   The Japanese allow the Dutch (and for a short time the English)
        to stay. The Spanish and Portuguese are driven out of Japan
        because they brought Christianity as well as trade.

1607   A small group of hopeful, but ill-prepared English men, women
        and children sail to North America and establish a colony in
        Virginia. They name it Jamestown to honor their king, *James I*.
        Thirteen years later another group of Englishmen will settle in
        Plymouth, Massachusetts.

1616   European trading in Japan is limited to Nagasaki and Hirado.

1634	Dejima, a fan-shaped island in Nagasaki Bay, is artificially created so that Dutch traders could be contained in one area and their activities closely monitored. This final restriction spelled the almost complete isolation of Japan from the West for the next 200 years.
1664	The French set up the *Compagnie des Indes*.
1699	In China a trading post is established in Canton and with Macau (previously established in 1557 for the Portuguese) these will be the only ports open to "foreign devils" till the 1840's when the treaty ports of Hong Kong, Foo Chow, Amoy, Ningpo and Shanghai are also opened.

Europe:

The *Baroque* era of art was in full bloom. The work of *Bernini*, *Caravaggio*, *Velasquez*, *Rubens* and *Rembrandt* was making an impact. This was a time of enormous paintings and frescoes and no great artist would paint a small object like a fan – but his apprentices might. Fans were almost never signed before the 19thC, so we will never know. Artists learned their craft by traveling from country to country, court to court. Copying some aspect of a greater artist's work was considered a compliment - not plagiarism. Somewhere in the mid-17thC, the French started to prefer *Painted Fans* to *Decoupé*. From c.1650-1730 *Baroque Fans* with elaborate subject matter (mythology, Roman history, scenes from the Bible and copies of paintings) were painted on fine vellum or heavy dark paper.

By the middle of the 17thC, the *Pleated Fan* was more commonly used than either the *Ivory Brisé* or the *Feather Fan* and had become an integral part of the wardrobe of any lady of quality.

As trade with the East and the Americas became established, the availability of tea, coffee and chocolate changed the way people interacted socially as non-alcoholic social functions became possible. Women could chat and gossip over tea or chocolate served in private homes. Coffee houses opened and male habitués in England began to form modern-style private clubs. With the advent of carriages and sedan chairs, people could move around with comparative ease. The theater became more accessible to women as the vogue for masks, full or half-face, enabled a lady to attend risqué performances without embarrassment. Fans, too, were useful for concealing all but the eyes.

Chinoiserie was at its height from the late 17thC to the third quarter of the 18thC. This term described Europe's fascination with objects in the "Oriental" taste which meant anything made east of Constantinople. *Chinoiserie* was often a medley of Chinese, Japanese, Persian and Indian style elements.

The art of lacquering, begun centuries earlier in China, was perfected during the 17thC in Japan. In Europe, the process was called *japanning*. Small lacquered or *japanned* brisé fans copied from those coming from the East, became very popular and were made in many countries. However, most of the European attempts to duplicate fine Oriental lacquer fell short, resulting in a lack of gloss and fine hairline cracks.

The art of molding and pressing horn was devised at this time. Once correctly shaped under heat, horn intended for fan sticks was placed in a cool press which set it permanently into the desired shape.

17thC Fan leaves:

From portraits of the period it would appear that *Feather Fans* were becoming less popular and were being replaced in court society by *Folding Fans*. On the new *Pleated Fan*, the leaf took up 2/3 or 3/4 of the available space and initially opened to 90 degrees or less. By 1650, fans opened to about 160 degrees. Elaborate subjects, often classical, Biblical or copies of famous paintings were popular. 17thC European fan leaves tended to be dark, painted with a central theme, with a heavy painted or embroidered floral border. The reverse was often painted with flowers, so the woman holding the fan could enjoy a floral display while presenting the major theme depicted on the front to the public. Fine goat or calf skin, often dyed a dark, purplish/brown was the material of choice for folding fan leaves, sometimes with the added luster of mica. *Leather Fans* were often impregnated with scent and painted with depictions of fragrant flowers. Thick dark paper was also used for leaves. Silk, which may have been used as early as the 15thC was not widely used for fan leaves till the close of the 18thC. Compared to skins, silk had obvious disadvantages: it is only suitable for one-sided fans, tends to crack along the folds and is almost impossible to repair.

17thC Sticks and Guards:

Ivory, mother-of-pearl and tortoiseshell were used for sticks and guards and were usually left quite plain. If decorated, they were carved in low relief. The 14-18 shouldered blades were not married in design to the leaf. As fan makers improved their techniques, sticks became much thinner with those supporting the leaf tapering to a point. Guard sticks became broader and blade-like, protecting the pleats of the fan. More elaborate sticks were inlaid with mother-of-pearl and tortoiseshell and in the last quarter of the century, decoration with silver *piqué*, a technique that came from Naples, became fashionable. By the second half of the 17thC, most fans had a guard length of about 12 inches with an open span of 180 degrees, with sticks more or less touching. By 1685, 24-26 sticks were common.

17thC Printed Fans:

The availability of printing gave rise to the first newspapers. In 1672, *Le Mercure Galant*, the first newspaper to feature fashion appeared. The application of printing to fans in the late 17th and early 18th centuries brought another form of mass media: inexpensive *Commemorative Fans* made for important events. Fan leaves, fragile, simple and often poorly made, were as ephemeral and disposable as newspapers. Engraved *Fan Screens* became very popular in Italy, France and Spain. Early master engravers of fan designs were *Agostino Carracci*, *Jacomo Callot*, *Abraham Bosse* and *Nicholas Noir*.

Germany:

Illustrations from a text showing fashions of 1629 show both *Feather Duster* and *Folding Fans*.

Holland:

Holland had a fan industry and was known for its *Church Fans* decorated with Biblical scenes. The *Folding Fan* began appearing in Dutch paintings in the 17thC.

Italy:

The fashion for *Flag Fans* was replaced by fans of feathers, parchment or other fine leather with a central handle of wood or iron. The most elegant had handles in silver or gold, decorated with precious stones that could be used first as fans and later transformed into jewelry. High quality straw marquetry had been perfected in Italy by the 17thC. An example of an early *Brisé Fan* with straw work survives in the *Victoria & Albert Museum* in London.

Spain:
Documentation by Spanish curators shows that there were fan makers in Spain in the 17thC, correcting the assumption that their fans were all imported either from Italy or France. Spanish ladies still carried the *Flag Fan* which had faded from popular use in the rest of Europe except in Venice where it could still occasionally be seen.

North America:
The *Westrow Fan*, a very rare, *Feather-mosaic Fan*, made in Mexico and dated to 1650 was brought to England as part of the booty from a captured Spanish ship. It now resides in Hants, England at *Breamore House*, the ancestral home of Admiral Westrow. The leaf, a mosaic made of Hummingbird and other iridescent feathers, shows figures from Greek mythology on the front and 17thC figures on the reverse.

In the book *LaSalle and the Discovery of the Great West*, an account is given of a visit in 1682 on the banks of the lower Mississippi River by a *Tasesas* chief who was preceded by two men bearing white fans and a third displaying a disc of burnished copper.

France:
France was becoming the arbiter of fashion in Europe and became the leading center for fan production. *King Louis XIV (The Sun King)* created the *Fan Makers Guild* in 1678. To become a master fan maker, one had to first serve a four-year apprenticeship and then produce a "master piece." Guild statutes from 1670 restricted the fan makers' subject matter, but artists managed to evade the rules by placing actual events in a classical setting. According to a 1679 statute of the newly established *Academie*, fan painters could not paint subjects reserved for the academicians, who were themselves arranged in a strict hierarchy, with portrait painters at the top. What appeared in paintings often influenced what appeared on fans.

From the beginning, European guild regulations forbade a master fan maker from making his own sticks. Those were purchased from the goldsmith or a *tabletier* who worked in mother-of-pearl, rare woods, ivory, horn or other exotic materials. From the second half of the 17thC onward, the *tabletiers* were increasingly located in the Oise region, around Meru. Very much a communal effort, fifteen to twenty workers handled a fan from the gilding of the leaf to the setting of a rivet. Each craftsman's skill contributed its bit to the finished fan's utility and beauty.

The Sun King liked to be represented in art as a mythic/heroic figure such as *Apollo, Jupiter* or *Alexander the Great.* Scenes from the lives of these epic figures adorned *Court Fans.* During his reign, finely carved and pierced *Ivory Fans,* similar to the Chinese imports were copied by the French. However, these were stylistically French rather than close reproductions of Chinese brisés. A common style had three medallions, linked by garlands and festoons. The ovals might display portrait heads or daintily painted landscapes and other scenes.

In 1685 *King Louis XIV* revoked the *Edict of Nantes* (enacted in 1589 by *Henri IV*). This edict had granted virtual freedom of religion and equality of representation, education and employment to France's Protestants who were known as *Huguenots.* They had suffered persecution to varying degrees by the Catholic majority and sometimes the persecution became very extreme, e.g., the St. Bartholomew massacre of 1572. Following the *Edict of Nantes,* perhaps as many as 250,000 *Huguenots* found life intolerable and emigrated to Switzerland, Germany, England, Holland, North America and South Africa. Many of these people were France's most skilled craftsmen, including fan makers. Descendants of the *Huguenots* can be found today in the American South, still proudly claiming their French names and religious heritage.

An extremely high hair dressing, a small cap with tall wired frills, was popularized in the last quarter of the 17thC by the *Duchess de Fontanges,* a mistress of *Louis XIV.* The style went out of fashion in the 1700's, but lived another day as a favored elliptical fan shape in the 1890's and for several decades thereafter as the *Fontange Fan.*

Because court etiquette dictated that ladies had to keep their fans closed in the presence of the king or queen, guardsticks became more and more elaborately decorated - often made of gold and inlaid with flashing jewels, so that even the slightest movement of a closed fan could attract attention to the one holding it.

England:

By 1600 the *Folding Fan* was known in England, but was regarded as an expensive bauble for rich ladies who considered it a status symbol.

The still popular *Feather Fan* appears in many portraits of the early 17thC. One shows the *Native American* Princess, *Pocohantas*, holding a fan with three large white Ostrich plumes set in a jeweled handle. *Pocohantas*, the daughter of a warrior chief, had converted to Christianity, married an Englishman, *John Rolfe*, and had her portrait painted when the *Rolfes* visited England in 1616.

It is thought that fans with painted leaves began to appear about 1660, the date of *Charles II's* restoration. Decorations were often classical scenes, usually spread over the whole leaf, with long, narrow sticks each painted in separate colors and designs. The first *Pleated Fans* opened to no more than one-third of a circle. By 1650, they opened to about 160 degrees. The leaf covered about two-thirds of the 14-18 shouldered blades. *Charles II* blades were deeply shouldered, widely spaced and sparsely decorated. From 1685 the number of blades increased to 24-26.

Catherine Braganza of Portugal who married *Charles II* introduced huge green *Sunshade Fans* to England where parasols were still unknown.

When Dutch *King William* and *Queen Mary* came to the throne (1689), fan making was already established, but they probably brought their own Dutch fan maker with them. During the next century it will be difficult to distinguish between Dutch and English fans as the fan makers of both countries used very similar techniques.

China: 1644-1911 *(Qing Dynasty)*

During this period the *Folding Fan* was not only accepted, but had become a symbol of status and identity, being used by people of all classes and as a medium to display works of art.

Chinese porcelain, one of the first important 17thC exports to the West, totally captivated Europeans. As fans were included in the shipments, they also became a coveted novelty. By 1699, records of The *East India Company* report that Amoy and Canton sold 20,000 fans for export.

An ivory factory was set up in Beijing and by the end of the century, by far the largest category of export fans was the *Ivory Brisé*. These were small, wedge-shaped and following European tastes, painted with designs and colors similar to those already popular on Chinese porcelain. Chinese *Imari* which copied Japanese *Imari* was made in quantity from 1638 to 1725 and early decorated brisé fans reflected this style.

Japan: 1615-1867 *(Edo Period)*

The *Edo Period* was one in which Japan was closed to trade and the outer world. During this isolation, the arts and crafts developed and flourished and most of Japan's finest fans were created. The *Ukiyo-e School* created many images of *The Floating World* of leisure-time pleasures such as activities of tea houses, geishas and the theater.

The art of lacquering, begun centuries earlier in China, was perfected during the 17thC in Japan.

Two great fan artists from this period were *Sotasu* and *Korin*. *Tawaraya Sotasu* presided over a successful workshop in Kyoto. He had a remarkable talent for utilizing the curved format of the *Ogi*, with compositions that radiated out from the center, conveying a sense of movement from right to left. The other artist, *Ogata Korin*, preferred painting on the rounded form of the *Uchiwa*. His circular designs were ideally suited to the format of the *Screen Fan*.

The Japanese made many different types of *Ogi* and *Uchiwa* – each with a distinct name and used for a specific purpose, ranging from practical everyday fans to those used in games, theater, warfare, as souvenirs and for a variety of ceremonial uses. Fans were (and still are) deeply imbedded in Japanese culture.

18thC – An explosion of fabulous folding fans!

Art in Europe:

The *Rococo* period in art (c.1735-1765) replaced the *Baroque*. It originated in Paris but soon spread throughout Europe, principally in Germany and Austria. Prominent French artists of the day were *Lancret*, *Boucher*, *Fragonard* and the deceased but still very influential, *Watteau*. *Rococo* was well-suited to the decorative arts. In fans this manifested as asymmetry, curving scrolls and shell motifs with light pastels and ivory-white and gold as predominant colors for the beautifully painted leaves.

Rococo fans represent European fan making at its best, with wonderful carving, piercing, engraving, embossing, repoussé, clouté, foil and jewel work on the sticks and guards and with leaves increasingly married artistically to the monture. The 18thC is often referred to as *The Golden Age* of the fan.

The *chinoiserie* craze continued till the third quarter of the 18thC. Drawings by *Jean-Baptiste Pillement*, pattern books such as *William Halfpenny's Chinese and Gothic Architecture Properly Ornamented* (1750) and *Sir William Chambers' Designs of Chinese Buildings and Furniture* (1757) provided inspiration for decoration on fans. These designs were not faithful reproductions, but interpretations altered to appeal to Western taste. Fans "in the Chinese taste," but not of Oriental workmanship, began to outnumber imports in England.

As the century was drawing to a close, *Neoclassicism* in all branches of the visual arts flourished from c.1780 till the first decades of the 1800's and roughly corresponded in thought to the *Enlightenment and Age of Reason*. Archaeological discoveries in Italy at Herculaneum and Pompeii in 1748 spurred great interest in classical antiquity with symbols of ancient Rome represented in architecture, the decorative arts and dress.

Rich young gentlemen took "*The Grand Tour*" around Europe to absorb other cultures as part of their education, a practice that continued into the late 19th and early 20th centuries. The 18thC tour route varied, but always included Italy and the newly excavated towns of Pompeii and Herculaneum. Souvenirs brought home might include statues, paintings and fans decorated with copies of works by Italian masters and memorable scenes such as Vesuvius erupting (which it obligingly did six times in the 18thC!).

This was a time of widespread interest in science and technology. Both the agricultural and industrial revolutions were beginning and together these two factors would radically change society. An expanding middle class was educating its children. Transportation improved with an increase in the variety of carriages. The stagecoach became a reliable, if not comfortable, public conveyance.

Fashions in Dress:

As the century progressed, the impulse for women's fashions was "bigger is better." This was exemplified by huge coiffures, buttressed with horsehair, cushions, wire and pomade. Dresses were made of heavy silks and underneath the skirts were hoops and extreme panniers (some three feet across). To hold their own with the big hair, big skirts and rich fabrics, large fans, ornately decorated and opening to 180 degrees were carried in the third quarter of the century.

Some form of lace decoration on costumes was still *de rigeur* from 1720-1770. Early 18thC *Lace Fans* heralded a trend toward textile leaves which would peak in the 19thC. Though surviving laces from the 18thC are rare, fan leaves would typically be made of linen threads, often with a coat of arms worked in the design.

During the 1790's fashion underwent another dramatic change, inspired by the drapery of classical antiquity. Light, usually white, one-piece cotton dresses revealed the shape of the body. In keeping with this new slim silhouette, smaller fans, better suited in scale appeared. Fan leaves made of skins were replaced by fabrics such as silk, gauze or net, embroidered with sequins and spangles forming classical motifs of urns, garlands, lyres and medallions. Guards and blades might be of pierced ivory set with semi-precious stones or of horn decorated with piqué. Since dresses no longer had pockets hidden under the wide skirts, fans were carried in the reticule, an early drawstring handbag.

CHARACTERISTICS OF 18THC EUROPEAN FANS:

Sticks and Guards:

Sticks and guards for 18thC painted fans were the most sophisticated and ornate of all time, increasing in elegance as the century progressed. They were made of ivory, tortoiseshell, mother-of pearl, bone and various woods - perforated, carved, painted, encrusted with gold and silver, backed with mother-of pearl or colored foils and finished with metal piqué work. Fans of the 18thC rarely had a loop on the rivet, but might have other ornamentation such as jewels (paste or real) on the stud.

In the early 1700's blades were either straight and narrow or very broad with no space between them, even overlapping in the gorge and with rounded shoulders. Ornamentation was complete on each blade and never carried over from one to another, but between 1750 and 1770, shoulders gradually disappeared and decorative motifs began to appear across two, three or four blades, gradually extending all the way across, permitting a wide range of ornamentation including carving, painting, staining, lacquering, chasing, piercing and even straw work.

By the mid-1700's there were 18-21 blades. These gradually became longer and more ornate, reflecting the prevailing French fashion of piercing and fretting, while the leaves, painted with scenes and vignettes, became shorter. By the 1760's, thinner sticks, spaced widely apart (*a la squelette*) gave a more open design. Ivory and mother-of-pearl blades and guards were often backed with thin pieces of iridescent mother-of-pearl or metallic paper. Alternating materials or contrasting colors were also used.

As the 18thC was ending, yet another variation, the *battoire* blade in the shape of a tennis racket or guitar appeared.

As the new dresses with slim silhouette became fashionable in the last decade of the century, fans became much smaller with thinner sticks, spaced apart.

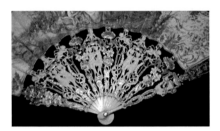

Pleated & Painted Fan Leaves:

By the middle of the 18thC, the *Pleated Fan* was more commonly used than the *Ivory Brisé*. High quality skins, painted in gouache, were generally used for fine fan leaves. Paper was used for printed leaves. Textiles were rarely used on leaves till the 1770's when silk appeared in England and France.

On *Painted Fans*, borders were often decorated with garlands of flowers and ribbons, while the reserves were painted with bouquets. After about 1715, pictures on fan leaves were often enclosed in medallions of gilded scrollwork. By the 1740's, central medallions in the irregularly-shaped *Rococo* style were the main feature on fan leaves, with scrolling framework on the sides.

About 1795, a new variety, the *Silk Gauze Fan*, came into fashion with the leaf no longer painted but decorated all over with gold or silver spangles. The ivory sticks for this new style were getting shorter and were decorated with silvered fretwork, as well as inlaid piqué.

Open Size:

There was a tremendous fluctuation in sizes over the course of the 18thC, from fans that opened to about 120 degrees at the beginning of the century, gradually increasing to 180 degrees or more, and then gradually growing smaller again at the end of the century. Within this range, very large and small fans were both fashionable at the same time. People carried what had sentimental value to them as well as the latest thing.

It was common for scenes from Biblical or classical sources to be portrayed with men and women in contemporary dress. This caused no confusion to the educated 18thC man or woman who knew these stories well and some are still easy to decipher. On other fans, the iconography presents a real challenge to the 21stC owner, requiring considerable research to correctly identify characters and plots in historical scenes. For some, this is part of the fun of owning old fans.

Silk leaves began appearing around 1770. Fans which formerly had the scene portrayed across the entire leaf gave way to different subjects contained within three medallions with round sequin or spangle borders.

Brisés:

The century began with *Ivory Brisés* from China painted in patterns similar to those on Chinese porcelain. From about 1750 unpainted but delicately carved *Ivory Brisé Fans* became fashionable and continued so till the 1830's. These Chinese export fans were very finely carved, frequently with a central medallion left blank to be personalized with the owner's monogram. Soon French and English fan makers were copying this popular brisé.

Inventions and Innovations:

In 1760, a mold for pleating fan leaves was invented by the *Petit* family of France, greatly simplifying the assembling of fans.

The first patent for making net on a stocking machine was taken out in 1764, marking the first step toward the mechanization of lace.

Printed Fans:

The fashion for *Printed Fans* emerged toward the end of the 1720's and by the 1750's, large numbers were in circulation. Mass production made these accessible to middle class people. Because they often depicted topical subjects, they have the added interest of giving a glimpse into historical events. Most of the 18thC *Printed Fans* were made by the simplest and cheapest method: etchings, often hand-colored later. Colored engravings printed from copper plates were perfected by *Jacques le Blon* (1670-1741). Toward the end of the 18thC, aquatints and stipple engraving came in, the latter a technique used by the Florentine, F. *Bartollizi*. Another laborious (and rare) type of engraving was the mezzotint.

By the second quarter of the 18thC, *Engraved* and *Printed Fans* were common. England, France, Holland and Germany were all engaged in printing fans and exporting them to one another. Now even the most modest, middle-class woman could carry an inexpensive fan. *Printed Fans* carried a large range of subjects and provided a look at what people felt, thought or were doing at a particular moment in time.

A popular example was the *Balloon Fan*. A series of famous balloon flights beginning in 1783 and continuing for several decades resulted in the great popularity of fans carrying printed and painted scenes of balloons.

From the 1770's till the 1790's a new fan, the *Cabriolet,* was fashionable. These were *Pleated Fans* with two or (rarely) three parallel leaves, so named because they resembled the wheels and spokes of a new type of horse-drawn vehicle with very large wheels. *Cabriolet Fans* of the 18thC had leaves decorated with a *cabriolet* being driven with the hood half up. Fans with two parallel leaves (but usually minus the *cabriolet* and driver) are still called *Cabriolets.*

Vernis Martin Fans:

Japanning, the lacquering of fans which had become popular in the 17thC, was perfected in France by the legendary *Martin* family. In 1730, they acquired their first patent for a lacquer formula. By 1748 they had three workshops in Paris, making furniture, carriages, decorating entire rooms and making exquisite small objects. Unfortunately the *Martin* family took the secret of their superior varnish to their graves. There is no documentation the *Martins* ever made any fans, but small *Brisé Fans* made from ivory blades, covered with painted decoration and then protected by lustrous varnish were (and still are) referred to as *Vernis Martins*. These fans, often finely painted with mythological or classical scenes, frequently displayed *chinoiserie* as a decorative motif.

Italy:

Flag Fans, though less popular than previously, were made with cut and applied straw. The luster and chromatic range of straw imitated gold and created pictorial and mosaic effects. *Straw Fans* were typical of the Veneto and Tuscany where plaiting was perfected in the 18thC. Also, reflecting the European interest in *japanning*, Venice had 25 lacquer masters in 1754.

In 1792 England's *Queen Charlotte* asked her son, *Prince Augustus*, who was residing in Italy, to bring her white Italian fan leather and fan leaves from Naples – an acknowledgment that Italy produced very fine leather for fans and that fan leaves were often exported unmounted.

Switzerland:

Fans by the painter, *Johannes Sulzer*, provide a detailed look into the dress and accessories of the second half of the 18thC in his native Switzerland. Other Swiss artists, *Jean-Etienne Liotar* and *Saloman Gessner* are believed to have also painted fans.

Sweden:

A domestic fan industry existed, but its date of origin is unknown. There was no fan guild, but fan makers and fan factories registered with different Hall or manufacturing councils. Laws were passed against importation to protect Swedish fan makers, but smuggling was a flourishing industry (as it was elsewhere in Europe). In 1744 *Princess Lovisa Ulrika* instituted an *Order of the Fan.*

Spain:

By the mid-18thC, the matador began to engage the bull on foot rather than solely on horseback as had been done previously. Bullfighting was to become a very popular subject on fans in countries where the spectacle was practiced. A museum in Madrid has a *Bullfight Fan* dated 1740-60.

Germany and Austria:

Between 1760 and 1830, Germans specialized in making clever *Articulated Fans* with moving elements. These were probably made by toy makers or jewelers.

1784

In Erbach, Germany, *Count Erbach* founded the *Guild of Ivory Carvers and Turners*. He encouraged local craftsmen to turn from wood and antler carving to the more luxurious ivory. Today an Ivory Museum in Erbach houses a collection (begun by the Count) of ivory, antler, horn, bone, mother-of-pearl, amber and tortoiseshell - as well as a collection of antique and modern carving tools.

1778

In Vienna the first fan manufacturers were listed in trade registers. This listing dwindled to a single name by the first quarter of the 19thC.

Lithography is invented by *Alois Senefelder* of Munich (c.1796) and by the middle of the next century, this new form of printing would be very important to fan making.

Hieronymus Loschenkohl (1753-1807), an Austrian engraver and fan maker, used advanced printing techniques to create *Topical Fans*, as well as *Silhouette* and other *Novelty Fans*.

Holland:

By 1734 carved and varnished *Ivory Fans*, imitations of Oriental lacquer work, were being made. These were distinguished by being smaller and often painted with a garland or small wreath of blue or pink flowers. Fans were in common use by women of all classes. They were used at court, for official events, balls, theater, funerals, marriages and in church services. Many fans carried Biblical scenes, especially from the Old Testament, but by the end of the century, carrying fans in church was no longer in vogue.

United States of America:

In colonial America, women were prominent in the dry goods trade. Itinerant sales ladies who attended fairs sold fans and other notions. Between 1760 and 1775 women advertised in the *Virginia Gazette* that they had fashionable fans of various colors, the leaves painted with the most beautiful patterns, mounted on ivory sticks.

America did not enter the China trade till 1784 because of British maritime regulations preventing their colonies from trading in the Orient. After the *War for Independence*, *The Empress of China* was the first American ship to reach Canton and returned to New York laden with tea, silk and fans. *Screen Fans* were especially popular in the U.S.

Russia:

In Russia, *Peter the Great*, who ruled from 1682-1725, brought in reforms aimed at making Russia more "Western." These resulted in the adoption of European dress and styles. Fans were imported before 1751 when the first Russian fan factory was set up. Then when *Catherine the Great* came to the throne in 1762, she re-introduced Russian dress into court and fans from her reign often depicted events of political and historical importance to Russia.

France:

After *Louis XIV* died in 1715, he was succeeded by a Regent, the *Duc d'Orleans*, who ruled till the young *Louis XV* began to assume power in 1723. The court moved from Versailles to Paris and this brought a change of style from the formality of the Versailles court. The break from the academic restraints imposed by *Louis XIV*, with his preference for fans heavy with royal symbolism, was replaced by the lightness of paintings by *Watteau, Lancret, Boucher* and *Fragonard*. Their beautiful people who played, picnicked and pursued romance in pastoral settings became the inspiration for paintings on many 18thC French fans. These fans, now more of a personal accessory, became an escape to the countryside for wealthy urban dwellers.

There were still restrictions on the subjects that could be depicted on fans and the *Fête Champêtre* did not become a recognized academic subject till *Watteau* was admitted to the *Academie* in the 1720's. Subjects from mythology had to be cloaked in some guise such as a play with characters in current theatrical dress. The presence of *putti* and flowers also served to transform a composition into an acceptable decorative genre. Still very much in vogue, *chinoiserie* elements often appeared somewhere on the leaf or sticks.

During the reign of *King Louis XV*, some form of lace ornament on costumes was still essential from 1720-1770. Lace making reached a high level of production, employing thousands of workers. But a few years after the death of *Madame Pompadour* in 1764, lace on costumes became merely a support for other decorative elements such as ribbons, artificial flowers and feathers, and was largely replaced by embroidery. Early 18thC *Lace Fans* had a leaf made entirely of lace, usually with threads of linen. These were a harbinger of the trend toward textile leaves which would gain momentum by the end of the century when *Silk Fans* appeared.

By 1760 the French fan trade supplied the needs of Paris and the provinces and exported a great number outside the country, with England, Spain and Holland being the principal destinations. Shipments were then dispersed from these points to America and the northern and Baltic Sea markets of Flanders, Scandinavia and Russia.

By the mid-century, there were about 150 master fan painters in Paris and an edict of 1776 united the *Fan Makers' Corporation* with the musical instrument and toy makers. This guild included fan painters, decorators, varnishers and the other small trades necessary to produce a finished fan. Ironically, the guild system, in existence since the Middle Ages, was soon to be overturned by the *Revolution* in 1789, causing the fan industry to go into a steep decline.

The south of France (around Grasse) became a center for the cultivation of highly fragrant flowers such as Tuberose and Jasmine. Fans were sold at perfumiers, evidence of the special synergy between fans and fragrant flowers.

In 1783 *Diderot & Alembert* published the ground-breaking *Encyclopedie Methodique Arts et Metiers* in Paris. This was the first time closely guarded secrets of France's crafts and trades had been openly and clearly explained to the public, breaking the silence of centuries imposed by the guilds. *Diderot's* work was among the first to express the *zeitgeist* of the emerging industrial age by encouraging the open sharing of formerly classified information.

The section entitled *"Art de l'Eventailliste"* shows the fan making process. The illustrations show women occupied with various steps of fan production, an interesting detail since the *Guild of Master Fan Makers* excluded women. One of the plates suggests by the furnishings that the work was being performed in a private home. The women may be wives, daughters or servants of a legitimate workshop as an *atelier* was commonly located on the same premises as the owner's dwelling and the room may have doubled as living space and workshop. It is known that many involved in the arts and crafts of fan making worked on the fringes, making fans illegally. One source tells us that entire Parisian neighborhoods where fans were made and sold carried on their trade outside the law.

During the *Revolution* (1789-99) fans were as much political statements as fashion accessories. There were patriotic fans that celebrated events in the *Revolution* and ironic ones like the *Assignats* that mocked the devaluation of currency. In the trial of the famous revolutionary, *Charlotte Corday*, she is recorded as having carried a fan as well as a knife when she stabbed *Marat* in his bathtub.

Revolutionary Fans ranged from 9–14 inches with 14-22 sticks. The leaf was always paper and always printed; sticks were made of bone or various woods. Many French émigrés settled in England and *Royalist Fans*, carrying pictures of the deposed royal family were produced there for loyal exiles.

The *French Revolution* disrupted the fan industry in various ways. First, it destroyed the existing guild system. Then the court was gone and the surviving aristocracy were now poor and unable to indulge in luxuries. Finally, it would have been very unwise for French men or women to walk around flaunting their aristocratic heritage or wealth by carrying an expensive fan.

England:

It is believed that the influx of French *Huguenot* fan makers to England around 1685 spurred fan makers to demand a charter. This was granted by *Queen Anne* in 1709 when she established the *Worshipful Company of Fan Makers* in London. This livery company is still in existence, known today as the *Fan Makers' Company*. Though presently their emphasis is on heating, ventilating, air conditioning and other forms of the modern fan industry, the *Fan Makers' Company* is an important link to the past, maintaining archives going back to their founding and supporting fan making in various ways. For example, they still produce *Commemorative Fans* for royal weddings, coronations and other special occasions.

Angelica Kauffmann (1741-1807), was an Austrian by birth who spent her early years living and studying in Switzerland and Italy. She settled in England in 1767 and became well known there as a home decorator, painter of portraits, mythological scenes and large historical canvasses.

Many of her designs were turned into etchings by the Italian engraver, *Francesco Bartolozzi*. A number of fans are attributed to *Kauffmann* and one of these resides in the *Victoria & Albert Museum* in London.

William Hogarth, the artist, was instrumental in the passage of the *Engraving Copyright Act* in 1734 which ensured that all British engravings, including fans, would be marked with their date and the name of the artist or engraver. However, this identification was generally printed on the border and was often trimmed off when the leaf was mounted on its sticks.

Though foreign competition was not a new problem, by the middle of the 18thC, fan makers were becoming seriously concerned with the competition of *Carved, Painted* and *Printed Fans* coming from the Far East and made several appeals to the government to tax and otherwise limit importation of fans. One effort to stem the tide of imports was the imitation by English ivory carvers of the *Monogram Fans* coming from China.

During the entire 18thC, leaves of English fans, whether paper or skins, were usually single *(a l'anglais)*, sometimes with the ribs on the reverse painted over. One reason for the single leaf might have been that paper taxes were higher in England than elsewhere. Often famous paintings were copied and the most popular motifs were Biblical, mythological or courtly. The English passion for gardens is reflected in fans that show wealthy men and women enjoying their gardens. Unlike the French who romanticized contrived rural settings, the English preferred real people in realistic settings.

Brisé Fans were fashionable from 1715 till the end of the century. They were made of ivory, tortoiseshell or horn, delicately pierced, sometimes with an armorial device – or with plain medallions intended to be filled in by the buyer. The English were skilled in carving ivory sticks and guards and, in this, competed with the high quality products coming from China.

Pompadour Fans, painted with works copied from or inspired by *Watteau* or *Boucher* and radiant with gilding and jeweled guards date to the reigns of the first two *Georges* (1714-1760).

From about 1730 *Church Fans* were issued with the sanction of the Bishop of London. These were painted in soft colors and decorated with Biblical subjects, pointing out a moral rather than illustrating a story. *Chapel Fans* from 1796 were printed with Psalms and moral lessons.

By the 1770's, fans were becoming less expensive and exclusive. Vast numbers of printed fans (often decorated with gouache) were made by engravers in London. *Printed Fans* offered the chance to present endless news-worthy or interesting themes cheaply and when a new idea caught the public imagination, the leaf could be quickly ripped off and replaced. Thus is attributed the saying: *"Off with the old – on with the new."*

The first *Silk Fans* appeared in England during the last decades of the 18thC, often with three different subjects contained within medallions outlined with sequins or spangles.

China:

Paintings from the late 18thC show that *Pole Fans* are still used in ceremonies such as funeral processions. By the early 18thC, the Chinese were exporting large numbers of (mostly) *Folding Fans* to the West. The Chinese exploited the intense new interest in their country by adapting traditional Chinese motifs with elements of Western design. They became familiar with Western taste as sketches, designs and prints arrived by ship from Europe and the Americas. *Export Fans* were not at all to the taste of the Chinese who preferred fans with calligraphy or perhaps a simple scene from nature done in two or three soft colors. If the calligraphy was a poem, it would have added value by bearing the chop (personal seal) of the artist.

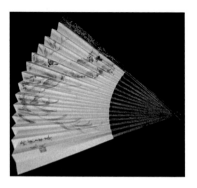

By contrast, materials used in *Export Fans* included gold and silver filigree, cloisonné enamel, black and gold lacquer, Kingfisher feathers, and above all, ivory, painted at first and later elaborately pierced and ribbed with carved guards. Various materials, colors and styles were sometimes combined on a single fan, so depending on your personal aesthetic, Chinese *Export Fans* could be seen as elaborate examples of exquisite workmanship or less than artistically harmonious - even garish.

Macau and Canton were the only ports open to "foreign devils." Traders were confined to *hongs* (large waterfront buildings outside the city walls in which they lived and conducted business) and they were required by law to deal with local *hong* merchants for all their bulk purchases. However, Westerners could buy items for their personal use directly from shopkeepers and it was from shops near the *hongs* that virtually all the art objects shipped to the West came. This restricted trading situation continued till the early 1840's when five additional ports were opened to foreign trade.

Since the *hongs* were the only part of China most Europeans were familiar with, they were a frequent subject on paintings and fan leaves. The *hongs* of Canton and Macau can often be identified in paintings by whose flag is flying on the various waterfront buildings. A fire in Canton in 1841 and subsequent re-building with different architectural styles also helps to establish dating.

Early in the 18thC, popular *Export Fans* were small *Ivory Brisés* colorfully painted with figures, animals, symbols and landscapes – similar to the decoration on Chinese porcelain.

In the second half of the 18thC, finely *Carved Ivory Brisés* became fashionable and large quantities were made for the European market. The finest of these were created between 1750-1830. Even the best European imitations lacked the delicacy of workmanship seen in Chinese *Ivory Fans* from this period. Many had three medallions with the central one, often in the shape of a shield, meant to be filled in with a monogram. Since the monogram was typically not carved till it reached its destination, many surviving *Monogram Brisés* still have a blank medallion. Debate continues as to exactly how these exquisite pierced and carved fans (and especially how their incredible, thin, vertical "threads") were made.

Some very rare, *Giant Ivory Cockades* were made for a short time, roughly 1795-1810. The cockade is not a Chinese fan type, but a European one, adapted by Chinese artists during this period.

The fashion for ivory became so overwhelming that Chinese elephants were completely annihilated and they had to import tusks from India, Malaya and Siam.

Tortoiseshell Brisés, much less common than their ivory equivalents, were also made. The skill required to carve this brittle material was even greater than that required for carving ivory. The rarest of all carved brisés were those made of mother-of-pearl.

Japan:

During the *Edo* period (1600-1868), the capital of Japan was Kyoto. Japanese ships were forbidden to go abroad, while Portuguese traders (the only Europeans) were confined to the fan-shaped island of Deshima and closely monitored. During this long period of isolation, Japan experienced internal peace and local artists and merchants flourished.

The *Edo* gave rise to *Ukiyo-e*, the *floating world* prints depicting daily life and urban pleasures. Print artists noted for their fan designs were *Ando Hiroshige* (1797-1858), *Utagawa Kuniyoshi* (1797-1861), *Utagawa Kunisada* (1786-1864) and *Kitagawa Utamaro* (1753-1806). The rise of *Ukiyo-e* and multi-colored woodblock prints, proved a tremendous impetus to the development of the fan in Japan. These new printed fans provided cheap, fashionable substitutes for painted fans. Merchants sold ready-mounted *Screen* or *Folding Fans* with painted or printed leaves. Customers could choose from a range of designs and have them customized with the sticks of their choice. Fans were also available from street vendors to take to theater performances where in both *Kabuki* and *Noh* dramas, fans were used extensively by the actors to accentuate almost every gesture.

In China many early fans were preserved when they were dismounted from their frames and re-purposed as album leaves. In Japan a large number of surviving unmounted fan prints from the *Edo* period come from sample books of the original fan sellers.

1793

A book, *Sen-shiki*, contains a number of legends and stories that relate to the fan with representations of genre scenes, pictures of old fans and an illustration of a fan-making shop.

19th CENTURY – THE CENTURY OF INVENTION

Europe:

All Europe was affected by the *French Revolution* (1789-1799) and the new century saw numerous regime changes. Periods of peace were frequently interrupted by war. Fan makers lost craftsmen and apprentices to the armies and navies of their respective countries. Overseas trade was disrupted and luxury goods from colonies had trouble getting into European ports. Many sought relief from the turmoil by emigrating to North or South America and other places that held out the hope of personal opportunity and stability.

This was a great century for the arts. Museums and galleries opened and proliferated. The visual arts were changing rapidly. The century began with the *Neo-classic Movement* and quickly cycled through *Romanticism*, the *Pre-Raphaelites*, the *Aesthetic, Arts & Crafts Movements* and *Impressionism*. The century ended with *Neo-Impressionism* and *Art Nouveau* which carried into the 20thC. Many of these styles were reflected in fan design and decoration.

Fashions and fans:

If, as has often been contended the 18thC marked the zenith of fan craftsmanship and artistry, a strong case can be made for the 19th being the century of ingenuity and invention, as well as finely crafted imitations of past styles.

Empire Fans of the *Napoleonic* era (1804-15) were called *Imperceptibles*, seldom exceeding 7 inches in length. In France, after the *Revolution*, there were no more Biblical subjects and few with mythological scenes or figures. From 1800-1825 fabric fans were small and delicate, made of gauze, net or silk. Leaves were embroidered with gold or silver threads in classical motifs of urns, lyres and swags or geometric patterns outlined in sparkling crescent, star, flower and leaf-shaped spangles. The monture would be horn or bone, often decorated with simple pierced patterns or inlaid with steel piqué. Most of the smaller 19thC fans had a barrel-shaped head, often with a circular, flat-cut steel sequin over the rivet. *Wedgwood* cameos of jasper, glass or jet on the guards were another innovation popular until the early 1880's.

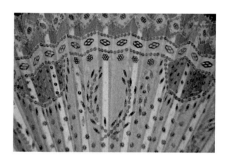

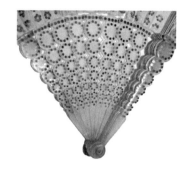

By 1820 *Brisé Fans* had overtaken the *Pleated Fan* in popularity. Fans produced both in *Regency* England and *Empire* France were made of bone or horn, pierced with a single pattern repeated on each stick and no decoration except for a few painted flowers and the ribbon.

For the first decades of the 19thC, women's fashions which had been growing simpler and slimmer since the last decade of the 18thC, now resembled a Greek or Roman column: the skirt was one long, slim pillar with a waistline that had moved up to just under the bust. Arms were almost completely bare with tiny puffed sleeves, simulating the capital on a column. Fans had to be smaller to go well with the slim silhouette of the dresses and to fit into a reticule.

In the 1820's there was a return to *Romanticism* which was reflected in the arts and dress. Taffetas, velvets and brocades were popular again. The waist moved down to its normal position and skirts became fuller. A *Gothic Revival* occurred, influenced by the novels of *Sir Walter Scott* and *Victor Hugo*. This was a nostalgic look back at a romanticized past. In England *Neo-Gothic* churches were being constructed everywhere and this interest was reflected in small *Brisé Fans* made of ivory, horn or tortoiseshell with crocket tips that resembled *Gothic* church windows.

In the second quarter of the century, skirts continued to increase in size and by 1850 were very wide, supported by crinoline hoops. To balance the big skirts, fan size increased. Trendsetter, *Charles Frederick Worth*, who founded a department store in Paris, promoted stiff, opulent fabrics such as satin and moiré with lace and feather trimmings. Fan leaves began to echo these sumptuous fabrics and trimmings. The sewing machine was introduced in the 1850's and machine embroidery, of a quality that competed with hand work, appeared on dresses and fans. Bright aniline dyes from the 1860's changed the fashion palette. It became fashionable to match a fan to a woman's outfit.

Changes in fashions were accelerated by new ways of marketing. The first department stores with the novel concept of fixed prices changed the way people shopped: *Les Grands Magasins du Louvre, Le Bon Marche, Galeries Lafayette, the House of Worth* and *Printemps* in Paris; *Liberty's* and *Harrod's* in London; *Lord & Taylor, Bonwit Teller, Saks Fifth Avenue, Bloomingdale's* in New York; *Marshall Field* and *Carson Pirie Scott & Co.* in Chicago were all in operation by the last quarter of the century. Even before entering these fabulous new emporia, their huge show windows (another 19thC innovation) fueled the desire for goods of all sorts. Shopping and even "window shopping" became a new form of entertainment. Women's magazines became very popular and dictated what would be fashionable in the coming season. Fans could be purchased in department stores, perfumeries and boutiques, as well as in shops devoted solely to fans.

The period from 1885-1914 became known as *La Belle Epoque* and the fan has been described as a mirror of this brief but glamorous era. In the last years of the century, the flamboyant elegance of fashionable dress was exemplified by an hourglass figure, firmly corseted, with a bustle now drawing attention to the back of a dress with flaring skirt. This silhouette required a large, dramatic fan to balance its lines and fans were an essential accessory at receptions, balls, dinner parties and theatrical performances.

During this time the *Morning Fan* was light and simple, a practical accessory. *Evening Fans*, however, were made to be admired. A *Lace* or *Feather Fan* with tortoiseshell, ivory or mother-of-pearl monture was appropriate for dinner. The guard was very important, perhaps set with sparkling jewels or an elaborate monogram. A revival of interest in the 18thC resulted in many fans with leaves painted with romantic scenes, mythology or court life. Another choice might be a fan in the current *Art Nouveau* style. Any of these would be ideal to attract attention and start a conversation at dinner parties.

Lace:
The *French Revolution* put an end to France's great lace making era because in its immediate aftermath, lace was considered aristocratic and nobody dared wear it. Under *Napoleon's* directives, French lace production began to revive. Later *Empress Eugenie*, seeing the effects of machine-made lace on the handmade industry, made efforts as well.

Machinery for lace making was invented in 1808 and machine-made lace came into widespread use in the 1840's. By 1860, improvements in lace making technology meant that acceptable imitations were turned out in great numbers. Production of handmade lace soon declined dramatically so that only rich patrons could afford it. Affordable machine-made lace was good news for the middle classes, but presaged the end of the handmade lace industry.

White Lace Fan leaves have traditionally been mounted on ivory or mother-of-pearl and if the lace is ecru or black, on tortoiseshell.

For the first decades of the 19thC, lace on fans was light to complement the classically inspired clothes. As dresses became increasingly heavy and ornate after 1830 (and with the lace industry recovering), lace became important again. *Lace Fans* reached their peak of popularity and also their largest size between 1880-1900.

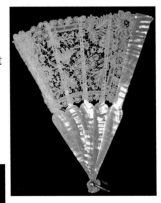

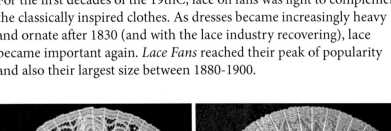

Some popular lace types used on fans were: *Alençon, Argentan, Brussels Point de Gaze, Burano, Chantilly, Honiton, Maltese, Mechlin, Venetian, Youghal* and *Carrickmacross*. Silk and cotton were the most common threads used for 19thC laces, but occasionally threads of metal, wool, aloe fiber or even human hair were also used.

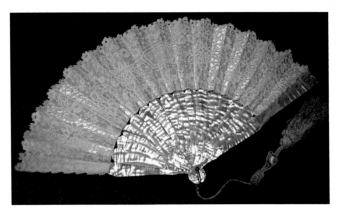

Feathers:

The "Queen of Fans," out of favor since the 17thC, made a strong comeback in the last half of the 19thC. Beginning about 1860 and for the rest of the century, *Feather Fans* made by Western fan makers were once again really fashionable.

In the late 19thC, countless birds were killed each year for their feathers. There was hardly a bird, particularly if it had colorful plumage, that was not considered suitable for making an entire fan or providing ornamentation on one. It was also not uncommon in the last decades of the century to see an entire stuffed bird perched on the side of a hat. Since feathers were costly, it was common practice for men to offer female friends the feathers from a hunt to be transformed into a fan or decoration of some sort.

For debutantes and weddings, fan makers in Brazil and Argentina made round fixed canvas fans on bone or ivory handles, covering the mount with feathers and (sometimes) the additional decoration of iridescent green beetle wings. The fans were tipped with Marabou and the centerpiece was a complete Hummingbird. Large numbers of these were manufactured in South America during the last quarter of the 19thC.

Fans of Ostrich feathers were among the most sought after in the second half of the century. To meet the demand, Ostriches were farmed extensively in South Africa. There were also farms in the U.S.. Six wholesale auctions were held each year in London where fan makers could buy three different qualities. At the top were white feathers from the rump and ends of male wings. Intermediate quality were grey and speckled brown feathers from the female, used for dyeing in fashionable colors and black plumes from the male. *Ostrich Fans* were often very large when open, exceeding 24 inches in the 1890's.

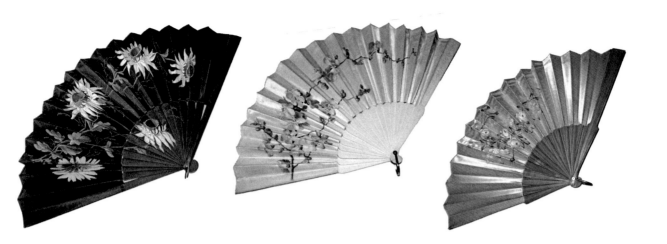

Painted Fans:

Artists of the 19thC produced many beautiful *Painted Fans*, often with the additional embellishment of sequins and spangles. In the second half of the century, flowers became prominent on fans, echoing the Victorian *Language of Flowers* (sentiments attached to particular flowers and colors). During this period "*Say it with flowers.*" was not a mere advertising slogan as it is today. Single flowers and bouquets were chosen carefully to convey specific meanings.

Western fans of fine quality were presented in boxes covered with leather, satin or brocade. Simpler, but attractive, sturdy boxes were made of cardboard, covered in papers that simulated fabric or leather. The simplest container was a rectangular paper tube with a lid.

Novelty Fans, first seen in the 18thC, proliferated in the 19th. Fans in many new forms, some practical and some quite fantastic and impractical, were patented by the hundreds.

A *Topical Fan* that had its moment was the *Giraffe Fan*, first seen in 1827, the year *Mehemet Ali*, the Pasha of Egypt, offered two orphaned Giraffe calves to *Charles X* of France and *George IV* of England. Viewed for the first time by Europeans, these animals caused a furor and their likeness appeared on many objects, including fans. Exotic animals like Giraffes and Camels were often comically distorted by artists who had heard about, but never seen, these creatures.

The *Fire Screen*, a fixed fan, enjoyed popularity from about 1830. This was not a fan for creating a breeze, but was intended to shield the face from the heat of the fireplace (and to keep makeup intact). Since central European countries preferred ceramic or metal stoves to warm a room, these screens were made and used mainly in England, the U.S and northern European countries where fireplaces were common. *Fire Screens* might be made of almost any stiff material such as cardboard, paper mache or wood. They were also made of various fabrics stretched taut on a frame. Fabric fans were frequently embellished with painting, embroidery, feathers, fringe and other ornamentation. Handles were typically 8-10 inches long and made of turned wood, bone or ivory. *Fire Screens* usually came in pairs and when not in use, they rested decoratively on the mantel of the fireplace.

Mourning Fans, first seen in the 18thC, became *de rigueur* in the 19thC. For the upper classes there was a strict protocol attached to various stages of mourning with appropriate colors brought out to mark each stage. The prolonged mourning of *Queen Victoria* after the death of her beloved *Albert* probably contributed to the rigidity of customs surrounding death and its aftermath in the last half of the century.

Hobbies and collecting had become popular pastimes of the middle and upper classes and one fan type popular in the second half of the 19thC was the *Autograph Fan*. Fans might be signed by royalty, artists, musicians, writers and other important figures - perhaps with a sketch, several bars of music or other artistic expression. Most, however, were humble fans, signed by ordinary people.

Another popular fan appearing around the same time was the *Monogram Fan* (aka *Crest* or *Scrap* fan) decorated with crests, logos, flags and other graphic souvenirs accumulated over time and pasted onto the fan's leaf.

A favorite keepsake that appeared in the last decades of the century was the printed card that was also a fan. *Card Fans* continued to be popular well into the 20thC and some reprints from the late 19thC are still made.

Inventions and Innovations:

A revived interest in decoupé led to a process for mechanically punching the leaf. Machine-made lace now made attractive *Lace Fans* affordable. The use of machine embroidery on fan leaves was another innovation of the second half of the 19thC and the quality was soon competitive with hand embroidery. In mid-century, a machine was invented for pleating the leaf. In 1859 the invention of a machine that turned out fan sticks, resulted in lower prices, but also in "look alike" sticks. All this mechanization meant mass-produced, cheaper fans, but fans of reduced artistic merit.

Loops attached to the rivet (for the attachment of a ribbon) to make the fan easy to slip over a finger or wrist were introduced after 1816. By the 1870's, most fans had loops so that with new dances such as the waltz where both hands were occupied, a lady could suspend her fan over her wrist and immediately have it available when the dance was over. Tassels also appeared around 1870.

At balls, it was common practice to provide each lady a dance card printed with the names and order of the dances with space provided for gentlemen to sign for the dance(s) they wished to reserve. Fans were also sometimes used as dance cards, some even provided with a tiny pencil attached with a string.

Signatures on fans were rare till the 19thC, but by 1870, fans, especially at the high end, were often painted and signed by well-known artists.

Substitute materials for tortoiseshell were developed with protein from horns or hoofs, processed with heat, pressed or cast and then given characteristic markings with chemicals. This was good news for the turtles who lost their carapaces to make countless combs, decorative items and fan sticks. If a turtle survived the ordeal and lived to grow another carapace, it might be unfortunate enough to lose it again, if caught.

From the early 1820's *Lithographed Fans* were produced in great numbers and from the middle till the end of the 19thC, most *Printed Fans* were hand-colored lithographs of an improved quality that made them widely accepted. Until 1840 almost all paper used for fans was made by hand, making it much stronger than the cheap paper produced in the latter part of the century. Beginning in the 1860's, chromolithography was applied to fans, on fabrics as well as paper.

Celluloid was patented in 1870 and continued to be made till about 1940-50. In the U.S., the *Celluloid Manufacturing Company* in Newark, New Jersey produced inexpensive fans of this new material from the third quarter of the 19thC. Similar factories in Europe and England were also turning out *Celluloid Fans* till newer plastics made *celluloid* obsolete in the 20thC.

With the many inventions and innovations came a proliferation of fan patents. This applied not only to fan making equipment but to new types of fans and hundreds of variations of existing types.

Italy:

The area around Florence used salvaged straw scraps to make round, *Plaited Fans* sewn into a circular screen and mounted on a wooden handle. These were used as fly swatters and to fan flames over open hearths. Italy had a long tradition of making woven fans of various vegetal materials and this continued with different regions making their own unique types.

Spain:

Before the end of the 18thC most of the fans in Spain were imported from France. A fan industry was established in 1802 in Valencia where it continues today. Beginning in the 19thC fans began to adopt the name of the king or queen who was reigning at the time they were produced.

1858

The famous fan maker, *Casa de Diego*, was founded in Madrid where it is still thriving. This house is also distinguished by its outstanding collection of antique fans.

Christina Fans were made from 1833-43 when Spain was ruled by *Queen Maria Christina*. They were strongly influenced by *French First Empire Fans* in format and decoration. They are sometimes smaller but typically open to 180 degrees. The leaf is paper or skin, usually decorated with a colored lithograph portraying a social event or celebration in a romantic setting. Sticks are of highly decorated bone, mother-of-pearl, horn or wood.

Alfonsino Fans were made during the last quarter of the 19thC during the years of *Alfonso XII's* reign (1875-85). These *Folding Fans* (often brisés) were strongly influenced by French fashions. Another fan of large size, opening to 180 degrees but bigger than the *Isabelino*, was called a *Pericon*.

Scenes from daily life including many *Bullfight Fans* were also made during *Alfonsino XII's* reign. The leaves were printed typographically or chromolithographed with themes from the bullfight and usually little additional decoration. The sticks were Bamboo or wood; fancier ones might have sticks and guards of mother-of-pearl, carved or engraved in silver and gilt.

Isabelino Fans were produced during the reign of Queen Isabel II between 1843 and 1868. They bear the strong influence of French 17th and 18th century styles. Like *Christinas*, they also open to 180 degrees, but are much larger. The leaves are usually double paper with brilliantly colored lithographs, showing scenes of history, court life or country scenes. Some *Isabelinos* are painted and signed by well-known Spanish artists. Like *French Rococo Fans*, the scenes are often enclosed in medallions, separated by *Gothic* or *Islamic* architecture. Leaf decoration, usually in gold, is heavy and ornate. The wood, bone or mother-of-pearl blades are long and wide with rounded tops and are disproportionately large relative to the leaf. If blades are mother-of-pearl, which was very common, they are flat, pierced or carved, usually gilded and often display *Islamic* design elements. Another distinctive characteristic of the *Isabelino* is its heavy weight.

Sweden:

Opera star, *Jenny Lind* (1820-1887) who became court singer to the King of Sweden in 1840, went on to sing for royalty and in opera houses all over Europe. The *Jenny Lind Fan*, made in many countries, is associated with *The Swedish Nightingale*, and her famous tour of America in 1850. Each segment of the fan is shaped like a large, wide feather, often tipped with Marabou. Feather-like brisé fans of this type still bear her name.

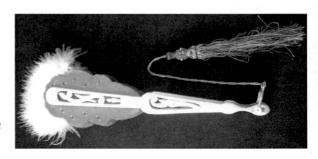

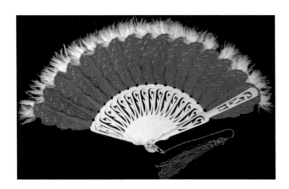

Switzerland:

Beginning about 1860, Switzerland began producing *Swiss Canton Fans*. The blades of these popular wooden brisés were decorated with decals of women in the typical dress of their local canton (county/province) and its coat of arms. Colorful and educational, they were interesting souvenirs of a trip to Switzerland.

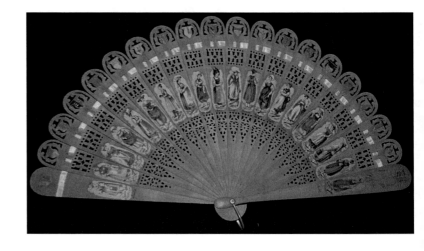

Austro-Hungarian Empire:

Fan production which had declined drastically in the first half of the 19thC in Austria, made a comeback in the second half. Vienna was the capital of the *Austro-Hungarian Empire* till the end of World War I (1918) and from 1873, the date of the first World's Fair in a German-speaking country, till war's end, many souvenir and commemorative fans were produced. *Wooden Brisé Fans*, often painted or decorated with decals first appeared in 1862-63 and were immensely popular till *celluloid* replaced wood in the 1920's.

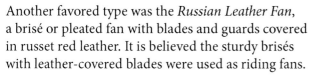

Another favored type was the *Russian Leather Fan*, a brisé or pleated fan with blades and guards covered in russet red leather. It is believed the sturdy brisés with leather-covered blades were used as riding fans.

Social and economic conditions in the first half of the 19thC contributed to a golden age of cast iron ornaments in the German-speaking regions of central Europe. Unlike other Europeans and the English, they did not look down on this common, inexpensive metal and encouraged production of decorative items such as candlesticks, thermometers, open-work bowls, watches, pin cushions, perfume bottles, portraits, busts, urns, vases, necklaces, earrings and fans. Items were produced in several styles including *Neoclassical, Rococo* and *Gothic Revival.* Of course *Iron Brisé Fans,* were every bit as impractical and even heavier than the Chinese *Silver Filigree Brisés.* Nevertheless an "iron lace fan" of 24 cast-steel blades, each 1/100th of an inch thick, worked in an elaborate filigree design with floral and architectural motifs with each blade ending in a *Gothic* pointed arch was a marvel of elegance and technical virtuosity!

1849

In Germany, *Conrad Sauerwald*, fanmaker, opened his *atelier* in Berlin with a shop comparable to *Alexandre's* in Paris. Between 1875 and into the 1890's, many excellent painters worked for him. Germany had a robust *Arts & Crafts Movement* which included the manufacture of fans. In addition to beautifully *Painted Fans, Autograph Fans* and all sorts of *Feather Fans* became very popular.

1863

The *Rodeck Brothers* opened a shop in Vienna, specializing in high end *Novelty Fans* and in supplying the needs of the gentry and nobility of Europe.

1867

After the Paris World's Fair of 1867, the art of fine fan making was re-established in Vienna. Gold and silversmiths worked with intricate tendrils of silver gilt and silver enamel on the guards of *Brisé Fans.* Fans were additionally decorated with flowers and rosettes inset with precious stones or complemented by enamel work and painted medallions. This elaborate ornamentation made them so heavy they became more about prestige than practical objects to create a breeze.

Russia:

In the 19thC the *House of Faberge* was supplying jewelry, silver and art objects (notably the famous eggs) to the Russian Imperial family. Though not primarily fan makers, they made a small number of fans with beautifully enameled and jeweled guards.

United States:

The fan industry in the U.S. had a short but productive run in the last quarter of the 19thC. There were probably never more than four or five U.S. factories making fans during this period. Perhaps the first was *Williams & Glad* in Boston, Massachusetts, but the two most famous were those of *Hunt* and *Allen*.

In 1866-67 *Edmund Soper Hunt*, who had been in the business of making fireworks opened a fan factory in Weymouth Landing, Massachusetts with six employees. He scouted the local woods for Hornbeam (gum trees), the principal wood used for his sticks. The first fans were made of light or dark brown linen mounted on simple sticks of the local Hornbeam, a wood well suited for fan sticks as it did not warp, took a high polish and lent itself to graining. The sticks were often grained to resemble Zebra Wood, marbling, tortoiseshell, etc. These linen fans were called *Summer Fans*. Linen and silk for fan leaves came from abroad. *Hunt* had to learn the art of dyeing, gilding, polishing, etc. He was an innovator and inventor, describing himself as "experimenting from morning to night."

He developed a process for making high quality imitation ivory sticks. His process was kept secret, but it seems probable that bone was the basis - boiled or limed, filed, whitened and polished on lap wheels. He may also have started with ground bone and mixed it with gelatin and alum, creating a product that could be pressed and formed in steel molds. Designs pressed into the material in a softened state show rounded edges and lack the crispness characteristic of carved ivory.

In 1870 *Hunt* also patented a machine for the intricate carving of fan sticks. A later invention not only pleated fan leaves, but also glued them on the sticks in one process. Another triumph for *Edmund Hunt* was his process of applying real gold leaf on his carved wooden fan sticks. The gold leafing was cleverly applied, under his guidance, by women employees.

During the *French and Prussian War* (1870-71) no goods could be shipped from Paris, so American fans from *Hunt's* factory sold very well. At the height of the business, *Hunt* employed many workers. However, he had constant troubles with his employees; they either left or made use of his patents, starting up their own businesses. Soon *Hunt* found that in a business subject to constantly changing fashions, profit was hard to come by. Machines had to be re-built as the size of fans changed. Clever as he was, he didn't have much luck or business savvy and the final blow came when he hired unprofitable selling agents. Soon he was badly in debt and the firm failed. *Hunt* returned to his fireworks and the fan business was taken over in 1876 by *Edmund's* brother, *Fred Hunt* and another fan maker, *Frank Allen*.

In 1885 *Fred Hunt* and *Frank Allen* moved the fan factory to East Braintree, Massachusetts. The fans made there were referred to as *Allen Fans*. The master fan painter for this factory was a German immigrant, *George Keiswetter*. His specialties were birds, insects, flowers and *Kate Greenaway*-like figures. He developed a technique of outlining and then laying silver leafing on his designs. *Keiswetter* married another talented fan painter, *Grace E.A. Ford*, who excelled in painting flowers. Among her favorites were: Pansies, sprays of Forget-Me-Nots, Roses and Apple Blossoms.

The company was known for their fabric fans of cretonne, crepe, gauze, brocade, silk and satin, hand-painted and sometimes edged with Marabou feathers - as well as machine-made lace inserted in leaves of gauze. They also made *Ostrich Fans* and fans of paper (some were *Advertising Fans*).The *Allen Fan Company* existed for 25 years, closing its doors in 1910.

Tiffany & Co. in New York opened its doors in 1845 and carried (but probably did not make) a wide variety of fans: *Eagle* and *Ostrich Fans*, *Lace Fans* of many varieties, *Mourning Fans*, *Vernis Martins* and *Painted Fans* on bone or mother-of-pearl montures. They also carried parchments for those wishing to paint their own fan leaves and various monograms and emblems to customize fan guards. In addition, they had a department for repairing rare antique *Lace* and *Painted Fans*.

While *Tiffany & Co.* supplied fans to the carriage trade, *Montgomery Ward* (est. 1872) and *Sears Roebuck* (est. 1893) set up business as mail order houses aimed at small towns and agricultural communities. For many decades the fans carried in their catalogs supplied the low-middle end of the market. The *Sears* catalog from 1902 shows a variety of fans in various styles and materials, with a price range of ten cents to $1.49.

France:

With the disruption of trade caused by the *French Revolution*, fan makers resorted to less expensive indigenous materials such as wood, bone and horn. The lace industry, a symbol of aristocratic privilege, was immediately affected and the number of lace makers decreased dramatically, though *Napoleon* made efforts to revive the moribund industry.

In 1827 the *Duchess de Berri* organized a ball at the Tuileries and asked guests to attend dressed in the style of *Louis XV*. This set off a search for old fans which fortunately were found in the shop of a perfumier, *Vanier*, who was also a fan collector. The fans were a great success and this event has been credited with reviving the industry of painted, decorated fans which had all but died during and after the *French Revolution*.

The area around Meru and St. Genevieve in the Oise which had become known for carving fan sticks in the 1760's was flourishing by the early 19'''C and Dieppe was well established as the center for ivory carving. Very finely and deeply carved guards from this area would be used by the best fan makers in Paris.

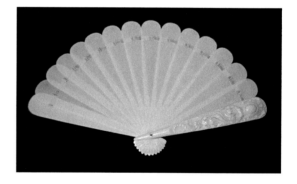

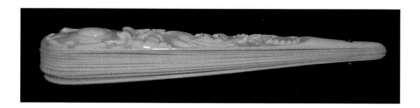

Specialty advertising using a variety of handouts was born in Paris. The first *Advertising Fans* appeared in the 1850's. One cooperative venture was fans carrying an ad for a particular perfume (sometimes scented as well), overprinted with the name of a restaurant, café or dance hall whose patrons were seen as the primary market for scents.

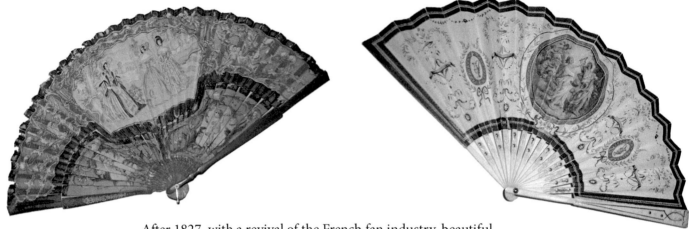

After 1827, with a revival of the French fan industry, beautiful, handmade fans were again being made for those who could afford them. Fan ateliers of *Alexandre, Duvelleroy* and *Kees* in Paris were established, employing extremely talented painters, sculptors, enamelers and jewelers to supply high quality fans like those turned out before the *French Revolution*. With nostalgia for the sumptuous courts of earlier eras, many of these beautifully painted fans on ornate montures were imitations of 18thC styles.

Duvelleroy and other fan houses also made lovely fans in a lower price range, turning out many finely *Printed Fans*.

England:

Queen Victoria (1819-1901) was very fond of lace and of fans and in 1839 commissioned *Honiton*, an English lace maker to make her wedding veil. Even in her later years, while in prolonged mourning, she wore lace.

Concerned about the declining handmade lace and fan industries in England, she made efforts to revive both. Disappointed by the fact that not a single fan of British manufacture was shown at the Great London Exhibition of 1851, she arranged a number of fan exhibitions. Though these were never really successful in priming interest, her efforts with the lace industry fared somewhat better.

Queen Victoria's husband, *Prince Albert*, was the moving force behind the 1851 London Exhibition held in the famous *Crystal Palace* (the first of dozens of World's Fair). These international events, held in many countries, would prove a boon to fans. Competing fan makers brought their most beautiful creations to be judged and awarded prizes. This led to cross-pollination among artists of the best designs and techniques. Additionally, countless *Souvenir* and *Advertising Fans* were sold or handed out at exhibitor's pavilions.

During the late 19thC, china painting and painting of undecorated fan leaves was an amateur art practiced by gentlewomen. Instructions for painting fans were printed in such places as *Cassell's Household Guide*. Some even made their own lace fan leaves and sent them to *Duvelleroy* or other fan houses to be mounted.

Human hair had its moment in Victorian society too. Locks of hair from loved ones (living and deceased) became treasured keepsakes worn in lockets or saved in small boxes. Hair was also used as a texile for embroidery and was woven, knit, braided and crocheted into a wide variety of decorative objects such as jewelry, flowers, wreaths, pictures and fans.

Around 1820, *Four-image Brisé Fans* of bone or ivory became popular. These showed one scene when opened left to right and another if opened right to left. They did the same on the reverse, for a total of four different scenes.

The Language of the Fan

Jules Duvelleroy, the brother who ran the London branch of the famous *House of Duvelleroy* published and enclosed with his fans, printed copies of *The Language of the Fan*. These were instructions for communicating with your new purchase by positioning it in various ways to send coded messages. This particular set of rules was loosely based on an earlier Spanish version. Over the years many versions had been published, adding to the uncertainty of the signals depending on which "language" you were using. *Duvelleroy* would have been well aware of the hold on the public imagination of a fan language and likely published his own version as a clever marketing device. Nevertheless, the belief that there was, in fact, a *Language of the Fan* practiced by those in the know, is one of the most enduring myths about the fan. Of course, even today, nothing prevents two (or more) people from inventing their own private fan language, if so inclined.

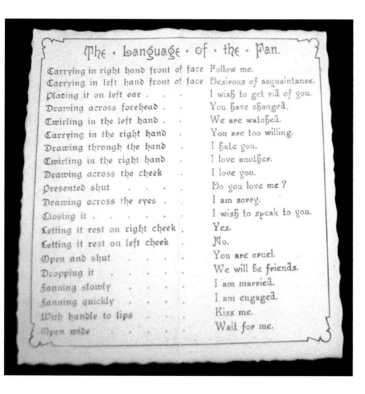

The · Language · of · the · Fan.	
Carrying in right hand front of face	Follow me.
Carrying in left hand front of face	Desirous of acquaintance.
Placing it on left ear . . .	I wish to get rid of you.
Drawing across forehead . -	You have changed.
Twirling in the left hand . -	We are watched.
Carrying in the right hand -	You are too willing.
Drawing through the hand -	I hate you.
Twirling in the right hand -	I love another.
Drawing across the cheek -	I love you.
Presented shut	Do you love me ?
Drawing across the eyes . .	I am sorry.
Closing it	I wish to speak to you.
Letting it rest on right cheek .	Yes.
Letting it rest on left cheek .	No.
Open and shut . . .	You are cruel.
Dropping it	We will be friends.
Fanning slowly . . .	I am married.
Fanning quickly . . .	I am engaged.
With handle to lips . .	Kiss me.
Open wide	Wait for me.

China – the Export Fans:

During the 19thC, Chinese artisans displayed for the West their great creativity in an array of styles and techniques.

A very popular fan from the second quarter of the 19thC was the *Mandarin Fan*, aka *Applied Faces*, or the (exaggerated) *100* or *1,000 Faces Fan*. Most of these were *Pleated Fans* with red, blue, green or purple paper leaves. Against this bright background, many small figures are seen, moving about in imperial courts or gardens with pavilions. What has to be seen at close range to be appreciated are the small, cut-out pieces of silk pasted on as clothing and the tiny pasted-on ovals of ivory, painted as faces. There were many style variations, including asymmetrical and telescoping and many types of sticks, including Sandalwood, lacquered, tortoiseshell, ivory (sometimes dyed red or green) and occasionally silver-gilt filigree or mother-of-pearl. On some *Mandarin Fans* a combination of all these was used on a single fan, resulting in the appearance of a salesman's sample. The Chinese sought to give Europeans what they thought was to Western taste – though it was certainly not to theirs.

Mandarin Fans from Canton usually had figures on both sides. The ones from Macau which were headed for the Iberian market were often brighter with silvered or gilded paper on the reverse, painted with birds, large flowers or harbor views.

Another popular export fan which appeared c.1815-20 was a white *Goose Feather Fan*. Some were left plain, but most were painted with birds, flowers and occasionally figures. Marabou or Peacock "eyes" were often used to tip the feathers.

Embroidered Silk Fans - delicate, sheer and feminine - found a ready market in the West.

Most quality *Folding Fans* were exported either in lacquered or silk brocade-covered boxes with interiors cut to fit the fan.

To store a fan or carry it on the wrist, beautifully decorated fan bags were also available. Some had thread embroidery; others had patterns worked in minute glass beads.

China made many *Tortoiseshell Fans*, both brisés made entirely of tortoiseshell, as well as the sticks and guards for pleated fans. Most brisés were left plain, displaying the characteristic beauty of the turtle's markings. A small number, very difficult to make due to the fragile nature of the material, were carved and pierced.

Carved Ivory Brisés continued to be exported in large numbers, however, with some changes: still finely carved with amazing, thin, vertical "threads," early in the 19thC, they began to be carved on both sides. About 1810 more people, animals, symbols, plants, oriental buildings and bridges were added, so that by 1820 they were always patterned with scenes from Chinese life - and after 1830, they were made with smaller sticks. Though there is no history of lace making in China, these "frozen lace fans" did resemble the airy quality of lace.

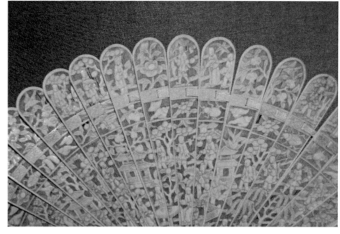

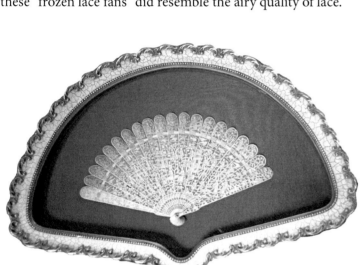

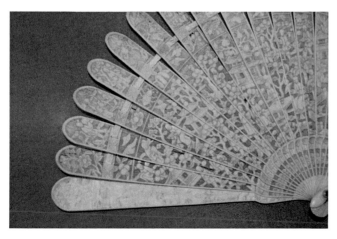

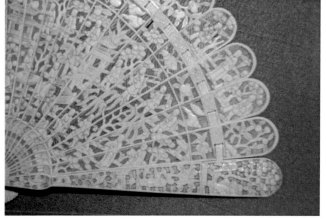

In addition to finely *Carved Ivory Brisés*, the Chinese also created *Uncarved Ivory Brisés* decorated with flat and raised two-color gold decoration. This decorative work was similar to the *takamakie* and *hiramakie* employed by the Japanese.

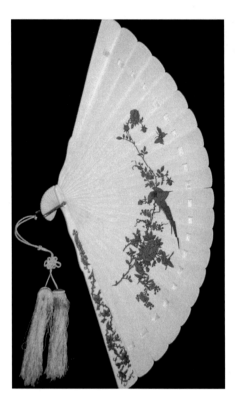

Fans of this quality might be presented in elaborately decorated wooden boxes fitted to securely cradle each one. Such boxes were themselves works of art, painted with two-color gold, enameled and satin-lined with hand-painted lids – a fitting accompaniment to the beautiful fans they contained.

From 1790-1850, small, *Lacquered Brisés* were made of light wood. Typical examples had a black background with gold decoration and accents of red, arranged in three distinct sections. A vine leaf motif was the earliest and most popular decoration. By the 1820's, a slightly larger type was made, still with vine leaf decoration, but now with scenes from Chinese life, as well.

Macau made *Silver Filigree Brisés* for the Iberian market from the early years of the 19thC. They were completely impractical for fanning and heavy as well, but they were very beautiful! Made by silversmiths and jewelers, these fans were sometimes made in gold, but were usually silver, gilt to prevent tarnishing and for decorative effect. The filigree work was often enriched with inlays of cloisonné enamel in shades of blue and green, with accents of white and coral.

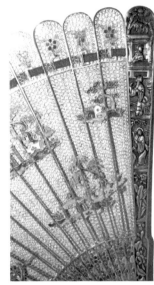

About 1840-1850, bone or aromatic Sandalwood became substitutes for
ivory, as basic materials for *Brisé Fans.* On many, piercing had replaced
carving. The blank medallion (to be filled in by the owner) could still be
seen on some. Carving had now became rather flat, with only the guards
deeply carved.

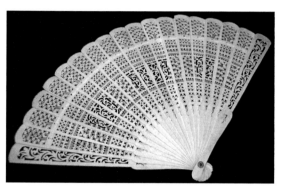

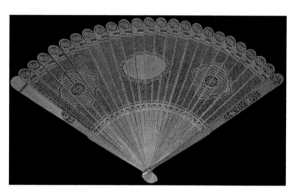

After the *Opium Wars* of 1840-43, trade was severely hampered in Canton. In 1841 additional treaty ports of Hong Kong, Foo Chow, Amoy, Ningpo and Shanghai were opened to foreign trade. Controlled by the British, the port of Hong Kong soon largely replaced Canton. Another factor, unrelated to internal disruptions working against the China trade, was Japan opening its ports to the West in mid-century. As intense interest in novelties coming from Japan took hold, China began to lose its market share in the West.

In 1875 the famous *Wang Xingji Fan Factory* in Hangzhou opened, employing many of China's great artists. Hangzhou had been a fan making center since the 12thC when it was the capital of the *Southern Song Dynasty*. This factory is still in operation.

Japan:
The first half of the 19thC marked the final days of the Japanese feudal state. In 1868 the *Imperial Restoration* was announced, beginning the *Meiji* period (1868-1912). The capital was moved from Kyoto to Edo (renamed Tokyo). In 1853 U.S. *Commodore Matthew C. Perry* arrived with warships off the coast near Edo. The following year a treaty was signed with the U.S. and by 1868 and the *Imperial Restoration*, commerce with the West was well underway.

Japonisme:
Japan's participation in international exhibits between 1873 and 1901 fueled great interest in all things Japanese as Westerners viewed Japanese products and arts for the first time, resulting in the craze known as *Japonisme*. The distinctive art of Japan (quite different from the arts of China with which the West had become very familiar) was soon reflected in the work of French artists: *Abbéma, Cherét, Corot, Degas, Gauguin, Manet, Monet, Morisot, Pissarro, Toulouse-Lautrec* and *Villon*; the Dutch artist, *Van Gogh*; English artists: *Brangwyn, Conder, Morris* and *Sheringham*; and U.S. artists: *Cassatt* and *Whistler*. New concepts of pattern, space and color emerged in their work, inspired by elements of Japanese art new to Western eyes. Most of these artists either painted their subjects holding fans, painted fan leaves, or did both, considering the fan's shape an interesting compositional challenge. Most artists left their leaves unmounted, painting them as an artistic exercise, as had Japanese artists in the 14thC. and since fan leaves were cheaper than paintings, they sold well. A famous example of the influence on Western artists is *La Japonaise*, a painting now residing in the *Museum of Fine Arts*, Boston. In this 1876 work, *Monet* painted his wife in a red kimono holding an *ogi* and surrounded by more than a dozen *uchiwa* hung on the walls and laid out on the floor. Used as decoration, the displaying of Japanese fans on the walls, mantels and in curio cabinets of Western homes became very fashionable during the last quarter of the 19thC. *Japonisme* was also reflected in the great popularity of the *Gilbert & Sullivan* operetta, *The Mikado* (1885).

Prints and fans (folding and screen) with scenes of Mount Fujiyama, figures in landscape settings reminiscent of *Ukiyo-e* prints and decorative scenes with birds and flowers were extremely popular. In 1891 fifteen million Japanese fans were exported to the West.

Japanese craftsmen responded to the new interest and demand for their products by making elaborate and ornate fans that showcased their skills. On the high end, Bamboo sticks were replaced with wood, ivory or tortoiseshell. Very fine brisés of ivory or tortoiseshell might be decorated with gold lacquer in high and/or low relief, known as *hiramakie* (low sprinkled picture) or *takamakie* (high sprinkled picture). *Makie* also appeared on the sticks of pleated fans, with insects a frequent subject.

Another distinctive fan decoration was *Shibayama*, named after a family who specialized in the decoration of lacquer *inro*. It was characterized by minute pieces of inlay in a wide variety of materials such as jade, coral, semi-precious stones, tortoiseshell, ivory and bone, carved and applied to the base so it would stand out in relief. *Shibayama*-style decorations often portray garden themes with flowers, leaves and insects on the guards. On some fans, both *Makie* and *Shibayama* were used to beautiful effect.

1881

The *Ishizumi* family established their fan factory in Kyoto. Still in business, they have galleries in London and New York and are active members of the international fan community.

The 19thC – a century rushing into the future

The century brought dramatic developments in science, medicine, technology and the arts. The Industrial Revolution changed the face of society, bringing enormous wealth to some - dire poverty to others and great demographic shifts. In England, entire villages emptied as people moved into cities. As public opinion shifted to accept social responsibility, the slave trade was abolished. Laws were passed to limit the hours and conditions of work for children and elementary education was made compulsory. Trade unions - quite different from their predecessor the guilds - but assuming some of the same protective functions, developed.

Communication took great leaps: first the telegraph from about 1830, then the typewriter in the late 1870's and the telephone in the 1880's. Transportation improved dramatically, becoming more rapid with trains and railroads. On the sea, steam superseded sail. The idea of public transportation in cities developed first with horse-drawn omnibuses and trams. London inaugurated the first underground train system in 1863. By 1900 Paris followed with the Metro - then New York City with its subway in 1904. People were on the move – and getting there faster and faster. The automobile revolutionized personal movement and as the century ended, the age of air travel was about to be inaugurated by a flight in Kitty Hawk, North Carolina.

Mass production of steel changed the way bridges and buildings could be constructed and led to the first skyscrapers, forever changing the urban landscape. In the U.S., those titans of industry who were first in on these inventions became immensely wealthy, aided by waves of newly arrived immigrants.

As the day was extended by the artificial lighting of oil and gas lamps, people had more time to read, write, work and seek entertainment. This was accompanied by a general impulse for self-improvement. Hobbies of all sorts and collecting became new pastimes of the middle and upper classes. By the end of the 19thC, electricity was replacing gas and oil and it was this last invention, wonderful as it was in so many ways, that helped sound the death knell for hand fans in the West.

20thC FANS – Western Fans fade away as
an everyday object

As the century began large *Lace Fans* began to lose favor. *Feather Fans* and the latest *Art Nouveau* styles were seen everywhere at fashionable evening events. *Ostrich Fans* continued in popularity into the 20thC, but by the 1920's had become merely a fashion accessory, dangled from the wrist by a ribbon - with the number of brilliantly dyed plumes now reduced to five, three or even one. No longer used to create a cooling breeze, these fashion accessories simply added a bit of flair to a flapper's outfit. An exception were the *Ostrich Fans* carried at very formal occasions such as presentation ceremonies for debutantes and by English ladies being introduced at court. This custom endured till the middle of the 20thC, but for all practical purposes, by then fans had joined swords as ceremonial accessories at formal occasions.

By 1910 a new style, *Art Deco*, appeared on the fashion scene. This was influenced by designer Léon Bakst's Middle Eastern and Russian sets and costumes for the *Ballets Russes*. These themes were picked up by fashion houses and well-known magazine illustrators. Favorite shapes for *Art Deco* fans were the arched *Fontange* (named for the 18thC hairstyle) and variations, the *Balloon* and *Shell-Shaped Fan*. All three have guards shorter than the leaf at its highest point.

Advertising Fans increased steadily in popularity, reaching their zenith in the first quarter of the 20thC when millions were printed. France produced lithographed fans advertising grand hotels, ocean liners, resorts, cabarets, luxury department stores, restaurants, champagne, aperitifs, liqueurs and perfumes. These were often designed by well-known graphic artists. Millions of lower-end *Printed Fans* were also made in Japan for the West to advertise resorts, restaurants, theaters, stores, businesses and political campaigns.

The United States, too, had its own companies that printed novelties, including fans. The *Ad Fans* printed in the U.S. usually had an illustration or photograph on the front with advertising on the back. They were often *Screen Fans* of various shapes, made of cardboard on a wooden stick. *Cockades* and new stickless varieties were popular too.

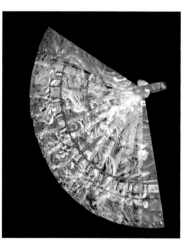

Many *Celluloid Fans* were made in the first half of the 20thC. Most were small brisés. *Celluloid* was a very adaptable material that could be marbled or made to resemble ivory or tortoiseshell, took dye well, and could be painted on or decorated in various other ways.

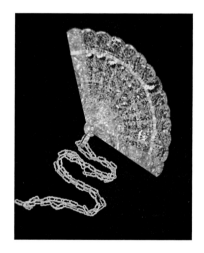

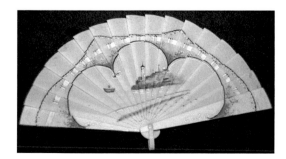

Another harbinger of things to come was the *Mechanized Hand Fan*. One popular model had three movable *celluloid* blades operated by a plunger mechanism. This palm-size fan actually did create a small breeze - as long as you kept pressing the plunger.

For the first 40 years of the 20thC, inexpensive paper fans handed out by businesses and political campaigners temporarily rescued the fan from complete oblivion by adapting to a new purpose - advertising, sales and promotions. As the century progressed, however, national magazines, huge billboards and, thanks to electricity, first radio, then television, became more efficient forms of mass advertising. By the 1930's air conditioning was being used in public buildings and though still far from ubiquitous, other electrically-driven forms of cooling such as floor, table top or ceiling fans were affordable and widely used.

Hand fans, still useful where central air conditioning was not available, were often provided in places like funeral homes and churches that offered *Fixed Fans* (usually with advertising) on every seat or tucked into the back of pews. Air conditioning was increasingly seen as the ideal. Movie theaters used this as an advertising ploy and beckoned to "COME IN OUT OF THE HEAT - FULLY AIR CONDITIONED!"

At the 1933-34 Chicago World's Fair, dancer/actress, *Sally Rand*, put fans on the map again with a dance where she playfully used the feathers of a huge *Ostrich Fan* to conceal her nudity. The Fair was not doing well financially, opening as it did after the Great Depression had set in. *Rand's* fan dance was such a hit that she is credited with turning the tide and making the Fair a financial success. *Gypsy Rose Lee*, another American entertainer also used large fans in her strip tease act. But aside from occasional reminders such as these in well publicized acts, fans were fading from memory.

During both World Wars, *Patriotic Fans* were produced. Many regular size and interesting miniature *WWI Fans* were made in Europe by the Allies. Fans that display flags can help pinpoint the date they were made; those lacking the American flag were made before 1917, the date of U.S. entry into the war. During *WWII*, U.S. citizens were encouraged to buy War Bonds and might be given a fan printed with a patriotic war theme. This was, perhaps, the last time fans would be used to stir "victory in war" sentiments.

It wasn't just in the secular sphere that fans were disappearing. The Roman Catholic church saw the final public appearance of the *Flabellum* in 1968. Following Vatican II, *Pope Paul VI* abandoned the use of a matching pair of very large *Flabella* on long poles, part of the papal procession that had been carried on all great occasions for many centuries.

As the 20thC drew to a close, Spain was the only Western country to still have a fan industry.

Was it electricity that caused the beautiful hand fans of past centuries to fade away in the West? That played a very significant role, of course, but there was a convergence of factors. The aftermath of *World War I* was a defining moment for fans as it was for many other "former things." Women were on the move and feminine hands now often held the steering wheel of an automobile, a cigarette or a cocktail. Having recently won the vote, their civic involvement was no longer conducted behind the scenes. Fashion was changing in ways unthinkable only a few years earlier. Respectable girls now wore makeup; hair was bobbed short; flapper skirts revealed the ankles and calves. The social scene was changing too. "Dating," not necessarily the same as courting, meant that women no longer had chaperones when in the company of men.

Unmarried women, often living independently, worked for their own paychecks. Though women working in restricted roles was not a new idea, the idea of women employed in male-dominated fields, a new concept, was slowly taking shape. "Rosie the Riveter" and other non-traditional jobs during World War II gave women a taste of what was possible. In the last half of the century, with increasing numbers of women getting university degrees and an influential feminist movement in the 1970's, status careers in male-dominated fields were becoming a reality. Fluttering fans, long a symbol of flirty, feminine, fragility, just didn't fit the new paradigm of "women in charge."

During the last quarter of the century, aware of the importance of the fan, an increasingly forgotten artifact from the past, *fanistas* in England, Europe and the U.S. somehow (well before the internet) found each other, forming affinity associations to enjoy the fellowship of other "fans of fans" in regular get togethers, visiting museums and other venues with fan collections, seeking and sharing knowledge - and publishing their findings. The 1990's saw the opening of three museums dedicated to fans, one in England and two in Europe:

An important event for the fan world was the opening of *The Fan Museum* in Greenwich, England in May 1991. The museum which is housed in two restored Georgian houses has over 2,000 fans, a reference library, a workshop for restoration of fans and a program of fan-making classes. They stage several themed exhibits every year, often with well-researched, illustrated catalogs. For special occasions, they also make *Commemorative Fans*.

The former *House of Kees*, a famous 19thC fan maker, was turned into a small fan museum in Paris in 1993 by its current owner, a fan maker/restorer. The museum houses about 900 fans from the collection of the owner's fan maker father.

A third fan museum was opened in Bielfeld, Germany in 1995.

HANDFANS IN THE 21ST CENTURY:

In 2002, a member of the U.S. fan community opened *The Hand Fan Museum* in Healdsburg, California. The museum offers rotating exhibits, has an annual American Collector's showing and conducts educational programs for school children.

In 2013 a fifth fan museum opened in St. Petersburg, Russia.

What has become of handmade fans in the West? Don't look for the spectacular creations of past centuries. Duplicating the fans of the 18th and 19th centuries is no longer possible. Laws protecting endangered species mean that ivory, tortoiseshell and many birds can no longer be harvested and sold. Once 20+ people were involved in the production of a single fan, but now with unavailable raw materials, lost skills and few people caring enough about fans to pay a single individual or small workshop to produce one, there is a very small market for handcrafted fans. That being said, however, a unique breed of artisans do still make fans. In 2010 two young French women re-awoke the long dormant *House of Duvelleroy*, aiming for a new market of women who appreciate both whimsical designs as well as beautiful high-end accessories. There are also a few independent and dedicated artisans who make fans for select clients who can afford bespoke creations for their private collections. One-off fans are also made for period films and special events. Sticks from old fans whose leaves are torn or dry-rotted beyond repair are often re-used with modern leaves replacing the worn ones. While still interested in the old materials and techniques, artisans experiment with new materials such as metals and synthetics to replace the high-end montures of the past. The 21stC world of handcrafted fans is a different world - one that looks both backward and forward.

Fashion and fans still enjoy something of a partnership. Designer, *Karl Lagerfeld*, is often photographed carrying a fan on the runway. He's been quoted as saying this practice arose simply because it is often so hot backstage at the fashion shows. Whatever the reason, it's nice to see a fan in the hands of a fashion icon. The pages of *W* and *Vogue* occasionally show fans in their fashion spreads, especially if the collection has a Spanish or Oriental theme.

ETHNOGRAPHIC FANS:

We have not yet touched on *Ethnographic Fans* which are an important part of the fan world. For various reasons, one of which is that they are not as readily accessible, these have not been as well documented as the fans of past centuries from the West or Far East. Nevertheless, many who have come in contact with *Ethnographic Fans* treasure their uniqueness, artistry and the fascinating ways some are used in their native cultures.

Since the word *ethnographic* has various meanings, here are ten characteristics of this word as it applies to hand fans:

1. Fans that, if found in a museum, would more likely be housed in the Anthropology section than in Fine/Decorative Arts or the Costume Department.

2. Fans made by people with a distinct group identity.

3. Fans that have (in most cases) a long history and are still being made.

4. Fans made mostly or entirely by hand that are either intended for the utilitarian purpose of creating a breeze, fanning a cooking fire - or as an integral part of the native culture and its ceremonies.

5. Unlike European fans or those made in the East for export, *Ethnographic Fans* always reflect the culture that produces them. They are not made to please tastes outside of the local culture, but to reflect that culture.

6. Though many fans made in the East are for the export market, some because they are made for a specific use in local ceremonies and events would be classified as *Ethnographics*.

7. The methods of production and numbers produced are typically small enough to constitute only a cottage industry and not a major one for the country of origin.

8. Local fan makers, realizing their fans are interesting to outsiders, usually make them in sufficient numbers to be purchased as handicrafts/souvenirs, so they may have become important as a source of income for those who make them.

9. *Ethnographic Fans* which would not be available for sale are those made for use only by group members entitled to own and use them (such as a Chief or Medicine Man) where the fan itself is considered a sacred object or is reserved for use in sacred ceremonies.

10. Despite typically using simple, locally sourced materials, *Ethnographic Fans* often exhibit a high degree of ingenuity and artistry, two of their under-appreciated qualities.

Ethnographic Fans of the South Pacific islands:

By far the most common variety from the Pacific islands are *Fixed Fans*, woven or plaited and made from abundant local plant materials such as leaves from Pandanus or Palm trees. They are frequently worked with designs (dyed or undyed) which beautify and distinguish them. The composition of Pacific Island fans is largely determined by whatever native materials are at hand. Typical are Coconut Palm, Pandanus, Jab (Hibiscus fibers from the Lo tree), Rush Grass, Cane, Bamboo, Straw, Lontar leaves, Coconut fronds (for twine) and light woods.

Some other styles are fans using shells as the handle; fans decorated with shells, fans with a tortoiseshell center; *Fly Whisks*, Goose or Chicken *Feather Fans*; fans made of tapa cloth from the Paper Mulberry Tree; *Folding Fans* made of batik-dyed cloth and fans made from the hides of Water Buffalo, Donkey, Goat, Oxen or Wild Pigs. Handles or sticks for these fans might be made of horn, Bamboo or other light woods.

Many islands developed similar ways of working the same materials and used virtually identical designs. Since island people were skilled navigators, it is logical to assume that travel and trade between neighboring and even distant islands resulted in learning from each other and copying styles. One author contends that fans made in the same parallel in the South Pacific Ocean, though thousands of miles apart, use the same method of weaving, e.g, Vila in the New Hebrides and Papete in Tahiti. Then in the 19thC missionaries carried styles from island to island as they sought to teach local islanders handicrafts they hoped would sell and become a good source of income.

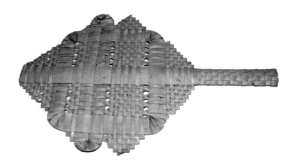

Acrae: Round or diamond-shaped fans are used for weddings or birthday parties. A similar style is made on Tuvalu Island.

Australia: Fans were made at a number of aboriginal mission stations. Missionaries taught aborigines living in Arnhem Land (northernmost-central area) and nearby islands in the Arafura Sea, Torres Strait and the Gulf of Carpenteria methods of weaving mats, baskets and fans. Coconut Palm and sometimes Pandanus leaves were the primary materials used. The string used to bind the handles was made from bark or the root of Wild Hibiscus growing on the beach. Missionaries brought the Fijian method of making fans to Elcho Island off Arnhem Land. The aboriginal men of Elcho Island made a *Fly Whisk* of Emu feathers fastened to the end of a stick with beeswax. Almost all the fans were plaited with designs woven into them - with designs differing from island to island. Today, with many made by machinery for quick production, the individuality of weaving has deteriorated, making it difficult to determine the place of origin.

Rock art of the Australian aborigines illustrates the use of *Goose Feather Fans*. They also used Emu feather *Fly Whisks* or bunches of leaves for their *corroborees* (dances), particularly in the *Mosquito Corroboree*. Aboriginal women make a fan woven of Coconut Palm leaf, closely resembling the Fijian shield design with the handle bound with a string rubbed in red earth.

Another aboriginal fan was made at the Mapoon Mission. Once again the Coconut Palm was used, the weaving and handle being quite intricately done, with the top of the fan finished off in a straight line.

Bougainville Islands: Round fans tipped with white or colored feathers are made.

Cook Islands: Rough fans were made from a piece of Coconut leaf, plaited. Finer fans (from Aitutaki) were made of closed Coconut leaflets stripped from young leaves. Fans of Raratonga are identified by their handles, carved with *Janus* figures (two heads joined back to back). Between the carved handle and the plaited portion, the handle was wrapped for decorative purposes with fine sennit (braided cordage) in a spiral, lozenge pattern. The wrapping styles for the handle vary from island to island.

Fiji: Here a beautiful fan is made from half of a pearl shell. Slits are then cut into the side of the shell and a finely woven Pandanus leaf fan is attached to the semi-circular top of the shell. A spatula-shape which originated in Fiji has been passed on to many other islands. Traditionally no one person could make a fan. One could make the flat part, but the method of plaiting the center attachment to the handle was known to only a select few and was always done in secret. The handle was covered with cord made from the fiber of the Coconut husk. These fans have traditional patterns of black arcs (made from an earthen dye) radiating from the base to the sides. A triangular fan made of Coconut Palm leaf, hastily woven, was used for fanning cooking fires. There were also various *Sunshade Fans*, including one 2-3 feet across with a flexible wood border that served as protection from the sun and rain.

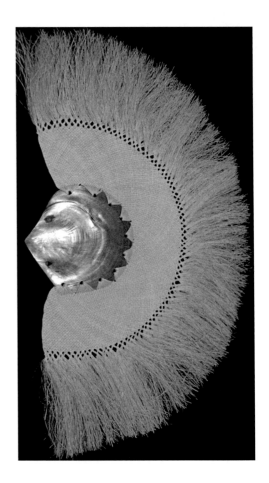

Tahiti: *Fly Whisks* were symbols of authority and the handles were characteristically carved with *Janus* figures.

Gilbert & Ellice Islands: A traditional round fan used when sitting in meetings or to fan babies and the sick is made from green Coconut Palm. Plain heart-shaped fans made from bleached Coconut Palm are made on Nikunau Island for the same purposes. Woven colored fans, round or tear-shaped are made on Arorae with a similar style made on Tuvalu Island. The older the fan, the more finely woven it is. Thursday Island and its environs make triangular *Coconut Palm Fans* and fans in the shape of a Maple leaf. Round, green *Coconut Palm Fans* are used in gatherings held in the village meeting house. Another style is a fan of Coconut Palm, woven in two distinct patterns, the top finished in a straight line.

Hawaii: In the past Hawaiians made elaborate fans for their chiefs. Some extant examples are finely woven with spreading handles embroidered with human hair and brown fiber. A simple fan was similar in form to those made in parts of Polynesia with the body of the fan composed of Coconut leaflets, plaited in a simple check pattern, gathered together and held with Coir (Coconut fiber), forming the handle. Another type, still being made, is the *Lauhala*, a diamond-shaped fan made of Palm strips woven with pin-wheel designs, zig-zag border and a woven Palm-covered handle.

Java: A midwife puts a newborn child on a fan as protection against bad spirits and to encourage strong growth. On a child's name day, the bad spirits are fanned away and good fortune is fanned in.

Madagascar: If a child is born in a "bad" month, a *Winnowing Fan* is filled with herbs to make the child safe.

Malaysia: Fans have been used in Malaysia since the 1400's. These fans follow the trends of Indonesia, made from straw woven into various shapes and sizes. There are also batik *Folding Fans*. Special fans are used at weddings during the "sitting in state" on a raised platform or special decorative wedding chairs. Male and female attendants carry the fans which are shaped somewhat like a ukulele, decorated with basic Islamic designs of floral and leaf motifs.

Marquesas: In the most eastern group of islands in the Pacific, chiefs carried fans as status symbols. Handles of wood, bone (or occasionally whalebone) were carved with religious figures. Some handles were known to be made of human bone (from enemies) and were regarded as family heirlooms.

Bali: In Bali, for centuries, the craftsmen of the island have specialized in exquisite ornamentation of objects made of hides from Water Buffalo, Donkey, Goat, Ox skin and Wild Pigs. Today pig skin is commonly used. An unusual fixed and carved fan was made from the shoulder blade of a Water Buffalo. *Wooden Brisés* are made of Bamboo or light woods, threaded with colored ribbons. *Wooden Cockades* are another Indonesian specialty. *Woven Fans* are made from natural fibers such as Lontar or Palm leaves, Pandanus and Coconut. Fans were also made entirely of roots. Another style is made of brown paper in the halberd shape, decorated with ink scrolling and *Wotan*, the puppet. The *Legong* dancers of Bali, usually three young girls, aged 10-14, use *Pleated Fans* with 9 sticks and batik mounts. The reverse sides are painted in different colors with gold scrolls.

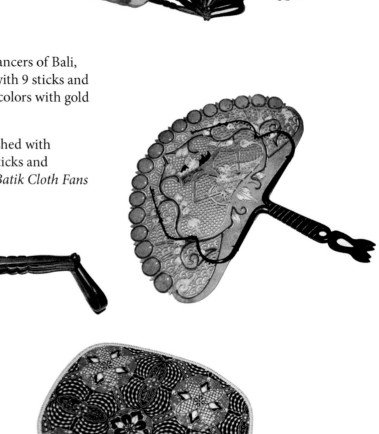

Both fixed and folding fans were made of hides embellished with traditional motifs such as *Wotan* or the *Garooda* bird. Sticks and handles were often made of carved and polished horn. *Batik Cloth Fans* are another popular style.

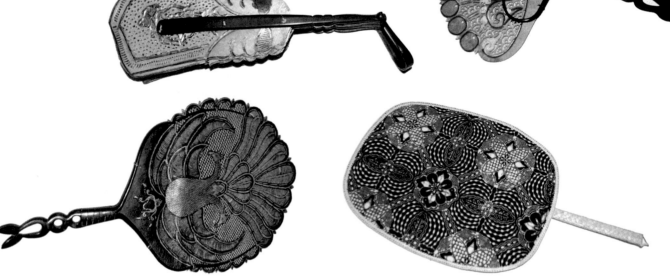

Marshall Islands: Fans are made of Pandanus fibers dyed in bright colors and crocheted in intricate designs. They are then usually attached to tortoiseshell with Coconut fiber. Fringes or Chicken feathers, plain or dyed, are added as the final trim. Handles are covered with Pandanus, tightly woven in beautiful designs. Fan materials include: Maan (Pandanus leaves), Jab (Hibiscus fibers), Malwe (twine made from Coconut frond), Atat (skin of vine fibers) and Kimej (Coconut fronds).

Melanesia: Fans are made of the Pandanus Tree leaf, formed in a kite or diamond shape and attached to a strong handle 1" in width. A very similar fan is found in Papeete in Tahiti. Islanders of Santo make a circular fan; its Palm strips are wound around Cane in a spiral pattern. The edges are then embellished with either dyed or natural fowl feathers.

Micronesia (Federated States of): Fans from the four states (Kosrae, Ponape, Truk and Yap) of the Caroline Islands are noted for their fine workmanship. Fans from Ponape are beautifully made from Cowrie shells, Pandanus leaves and feathers, held together with Pandanus fiber and finished with brightly colored Chicken feathers. Others have a tortoiseshell center, sanded smooth and thin, with holes cut at intervals for attaching the fiber framework of the fan. Kosrae fans are exquisitely woven of finely spliced Pandanus fiber usually in shades of black and white. Truk fans have an oval shape, dyed in various colors, with a pattern crocheted in the center. Fan handles on the various islands of Micronesia are covered with Pandanus fiber in intricately woven designs.

New Guinea: Older fans were open-work, spatula-shaped fans made of natural and colored Palm with a semi-circular top. Newer fans are round and plaited with a design going in a graded circle with the edges tipped with white fowl feathers. In the 19thC, fans were made of Bird of Paradise feathers, a bird now fully protected. Another beautiful fan is finely woven of Raffia on a handle of Abalone shell.

New Zealand: The southernmost group of islands being cooler than the rest of the Pacific Islands, fans were not required for cooling. They were used during the *Maori tangi*, a traditional lying-in of a corpse for some days after death as a mark of respect. A new fan was made for each *tangi*. The handle was wood with a smaller piece of wood laid across, forming a cross onto which pieces of scraped flax were bound in a lozenge shape.

Philippines: An unusual native fan is a *Mourning Fan* used by the *Ifugao* tribe, indigenous people living in a remote area who have resisted Westernization and acculturation for centuries. The fan is almost 22" long, including the handle. The main part is made of woven, Cane-like fibers with an attached *Bulul*, a small carved figure symbolizing the *Ifugao* rice god or guardian spirit. The *Ifugao* dead were sat upright on a Bamboo chair for a period of 2 days to 2 weeks while mourning was observed. The waving of the fan conveys a blessing to the dead person (as well as freshening the air around the body).

Fans from the Philippines reflect both the 300 years of Spanish occupation and the crafts and skills of the East. An example is a *Folding Fan* made of Piña cloth from the fiber of the Pineapple plant, either plain or in colors and embroidered. Sticks are heavy, carved octagonally, rather than with the rounded carving of Spain. Several types of *Screen Fans* are made from the woven Burri Palm, beautifully finished with Raffia embroidery. This work is often done by children as a cottage industry after the day's work is done. Another type is a spade-shaped fan made of Burri Palm on one side and Banana bark on the other with a Rattan Cane handle. Crescent-shaped fans of plaited Burri Palm, woven in strips, ranging from hand-size to enormous decorative ones are also made. Still another style is made from Burri Palm, sometimes left plain, sometimes dyed in brilliant colors. The fan is woven in a spiral pattern while the plant is still soft and green.

The *Baranggay* dancers of the Philippines use brightly colored fans of light material with edges covered in sequins. They manipulate the fans singly and in pairs so swiftly it appears as if an electric fan is whirling in front of your eyes.

Samoa: Guests are fanned by female attendants who are also keeping flies off the food. A *Fly Whisk* was part of a chief's regalia. The talking chief or orator's *Fly Whisk* had a short, thick handle which he carried in his left hand, balanced over his left shoulder when speaking in public. Another type is a spade-shaped Bast fan, woven with open work, tipped with dyed feathers and attached to a woven handle.

Solomon Islands: Older fans from this area were kite-shaped, sometimes with the top squared and leaving a zig-zag edge. In the early 20thC fans were made in the spatula-shape with a long handle, the center very intricately woven and criss-crossed with the edge finished with open-work plait. Fans were as large as 18" in length. Another type is made from Akkar-wangi (aromatic roots) on a Bamboo frame.

Tonga: Older *Woven Fans* from Tonga are spatula-shaped. Modern fans have centers of tapa cloth (made from the inner bark of the Paper Mulberry Tree), painted with traditional designs.

SOUTH EAST ASIA

Thailand. A spade-shaped fan is made of parchment stretched over a frame of Bamboo. Two round holes are cut at the bottom.

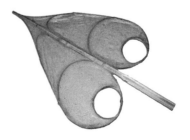

NORTH, CENTRAL & SOUTH AMERICA

Native Americans of the *Ojibwa*, *Huron*, *Iroquois* and other northern tribes made *Screen Fans* on birch bark handles decorated with quillwork embroidery. The mount was covered with assorted feathers with an entire small bird in the center.

Navajo and other Native Americans of the Plains make *Feather Fans* for use in their peyote ceremonies. The feathers come from a wide variety of birds, each symbolizing various spiritual qualities, with different colored feathers having specific meanings. *Peyote Feather Fans* are made in three types: flat screen, drop fans and swivel fans. In addition to the featherwork, the process of producing a *Peyote Fan* includes leatherwork, threadwork and beadwork in geometric, floral and other designs, frequently inspired by different aspects of nature. *Peyote Fans*, rich with historic and symbolic significance, vary in design from tribe to tribe. The North American deification of peyote is a very ancient practice. Peyote buttons found in a cave in southern Texas have been radiocarbon-dated to 5,000 B.C. and the *Huichol* Indians of northwestern Mexico were known to make peyote pilgrimages as early as 200 A.D., a custom still followed.

Smudge Fans are also still used by medicine men to move the smoke of smoldering sage packets and incense during healing, centering, cleansing and "combing out" activities (to remove energy blockages and negativities).

Fans are made for use while dancing in secular ceremonial gatherings (powwows). In a healing dance performed by *Ojibwa*s of the North Plains, female dancers perform the Jingle Dress Dance. A girl wearing a dress covered with metal cones uses a feather fan to spread prayers into the four directions. *Seneca* tribe dancers use *Fixed Eagle Feather Fans* in their dances. *Fixed Turkey Feather Fans* are also used at powwows.

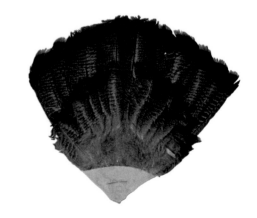

Inuit of Alaska make round *Dance/Finger Fans*. Large fans are made from very fine grasses using a coiled basketry technique, fringed with long White Wolf hair.

In another smaller version, there is a central medallion of Caribou skin, painted with a face surrounded by a small fur ruff. A finger loop is attached above the top of the face. The dancer hooks his fingers through a loop in the fans. With a fan on each hand, the dancer uses the fan as an extension of his arms as he dips and sways.

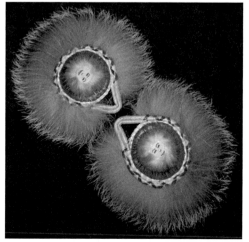

Mexicans in rural villages make a *Sopledor* or *Fire Fan* to increase the heat of cooking fires. These are small fans made of plaited grasses. They also make fans with a plywood handle punched with holes near the top to which grasses are attached and woven to form the leaf. Another variety is made from strips of plaited grasses, machine-stitched in a circle with a corn husk flower decorating the center. The round screen is affixed to a Bamboo handle.

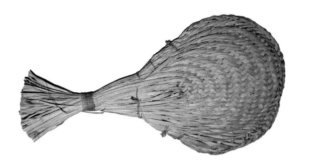

Guatemalans make a diamond-shaped *Screen Fan* decorated with colorful woven cotton ribbons, a doll figure and straw baskets. The handle is a sheaf of Palustrine grass.

South America:

In the tropical forests of South America fans are used for fanning fires or are used as spatulas to turn cassava bread on griddles.

Guyana: *Fire Fans* are made of reeds or Palm leaves. Because of their beliefs fans are not used for cooling themselves or dispatching insects. Cooling is accomplished by frequent bathing; mosquitoes are kept off by rubbing their bodies with mud or Crabwood and by the use of smoky fires under their hammocks at night.

Peru: The *Yaqua* Indians make fixed fans of woven Palm, decorated with colored fish scales and beads of berries.

Brazil: One fan type is made of pressed root with a zig-zag border of plaited Palm leaf.

AFRICA

The *Fly Whisk* was intended to protect the king from insects and the parasol to provide protection from the elements. Both are commonly found in African courts. In many societies the use of the *Fly Whisk* was the sole privilege of the ruler. These were made from a long tuft of animal hair, attached to a wooden, metal or ivory handle. During the 19thC models of extreme luxury were made with hair from an Elephant's tail attached to a gold-leaf handle. Another 19thC type, very much like a *Screen Fan* had a leather plate with a handle carved with geometric designs or in the shape of a human figure.

Benin: The *Oba* (king) uses a *Fly Whisk* as symbol of his office and has a special whisk made of coral beads believed to be endowed with such power that whatever is said while the king holds it will come to pass. Craftsmen also made round leather fans for the royal family and other high-ranking chiefs. These were similar to those used by the *Hausa* of West Africa and the *Yoruba* people. They were made of cowhide or buckskin with appliqué designs in red cloth stitched with Antelope thread. Special designs were appropriate to particular ranks. The Queen Mother, as a symbol of her office, carried a round fan of wood carved with proverbs. At her funeral, her son would erect a special altar with a figure of his mother, attended by her female servants holding shields or fans above her head.

Leather and beaten brass fans were carried by ordinary people. One of these brass fans from the 19thC resides in the *Pitt Rivers Museum* in Oxford, England where many older *Ethnographic Fans* may be viewed.

Burkina Faso. A shovel-shaped fan of colorful, twisted grass threads is woven in various patterns. A very similar fan is also made in Ghana.

Cameroon: In the chiefdom of *Bandjoun*, in ceremonial dances, eligible warriors carry large, long hair *Fly Whisks* with intricately colored bead decoration, incorporating symbolic animal and plant designs. Their regalia includes very large hats, masks, ear flaps, a fringed cape and multiple ivory bracelets.

East Africa: A *Maasai* bridegroom in southern Kenya and northern Tanzania carries a hair *Fly Whisk*.

Egypt: *Flag Fans* have been made in Egypt for many centuries. One of the many uses is to cool a sleeping infant. Typical is heavy cotton yarn woven into a pattern with a fringed edge. Palm leaf fans with beaded handles are also made.

Ghana: *Ashanti* craftsmen make *Fly Whisks* and fans in brass. *Fly Whisks* were generally used by royalty, witch doctors and devil dancers. A colorful, shovel-shaped grass fan is another type.

Kenya: A witchdoctor's *Fly Whisk* has a hollow bone handle to contain poison. A prospective *Maasai* groom, attired in earrings and necklace, carries a hair *Fly Whisk* when he goes to the prospective bride's family to offer gifts (if the marriage proposal is accepted).

Libya: *Flag Fans* are common. An early example from c.1800 is woven straw attached to a silver handle with repoussé decoration.

Nigeria: The *Yoruba* make beaded, round fans and use Zebra tail *Fly Whisks* with carved ivory handles in their tribal dances.

Southern Africa: Among the *Xhosa*-speaking nations, diviners use staffs with whisks on the ends in dance rituals. The handles of the whisks have intricate beaded adornment.

Sudan: Examples of *Flag Fans* and Giraffe tail and bone *Fly Whisks* from the *Baggarta* are in the *Pitt Rivers Museum*.

Tanzania: Kudu tail *Fly Whisks* are made by the *Moshi*.

Tunisia: Dyed straw *Screen Fans* are common.

Zaire: Northern Zaire dancers use wooden-handled hair *Fly Whisks*. The chief's *Fly Whisk* which is believed to have magical powers to ward off evil is made of wood, skin, Buffalo tail hair and cord. The handle is carved with a two-faced head.

Zanzibar: A *Fly Whisk* is used by the devil dancer to summon the spirit world.

Zimbabwe: A Wildebeest tail *Fly Whisk* with a wire-bound handle is used.

West Africa: The *Hausa* people make cowhide fans. Some are *Cockades* with wooden handles.

INDIA

Many styles of *Flag Fans* are popular throughout India. *Fire Fans* are still in common use by street food vendors who use them to fan the flames of their stoves. Many hand fans were made as part of the dowry textiles a bride was required to have and in some cases fans were used in the marriage ceremony. Fans for common people were often made of embroidered cotton or silk stretched over a woven Cane frame.

In the past, a large *pankhā* (or *punkha*) was suspended from the ceiling and operated by a *punkawallah* pulling a cord to swing it back and forth. These large *Swinging Fans* can also be seen in some restored antebellum homes in the American south.

Very small fans were used in religious ceremonies as a gift to the god or to keep flies off an idol.

One *Flag Fan* is made of a single Palm leaf, bent and side-mounted to its stem which forms the handle. The border is made of plaited Palm leaf in a zig-zag pattern. Many variations of this fan made from a single leaf and stem exist.

There are also large elaborate *Court Fans*, often made of Khus Khus aromatic root which can be sprinkled with water to give off a scented breeze. Other *Court Fans* were made of mica, woven ivory and silver, leather or Sandalwood.

Fans were also made of silk or velvet, often embroidered with *mochi* (chain stitches worked with a very fine crochet hook). This is similar to Western tambour work, but worked on the right side so that the chain stitch shows. Other embroidery stitches are satin and herringbone, often applied with *shisha* (pieces of mirror to ward off the evil eye). Decorative techniques include appliqué, *zari* (gold work) and *gota* (gold and silver ribbon work). Handles may be covered with fabric, made of ivory or of lacquered wood, turned and carved.

The *Gossip Fan* was a large, axe-shaped fan held by a woman sitting in the center of a group. This fan was twirled in a circle, thus fanning an entire group of people at the same time.

Gujarat: In this area of India, half circle/axe-shaped fans on turned sticks are used by herders and other pastoral workers. Examples are beaded all over except for the frills around the edges. Beadwork fans are made with a frame and a stiffened backing, using a netting technique. The designs on embroidered fans, especially for the herders, are similar to those on their dress and through symbolism and color express their identity and status in society. In some interior parts of central Gujarat, these fans are made of leather, cut into an axe shape with turned and colored wooden handles. Patches of small geometrical designs in different colored leather are sewn on. These fans are made to be twirled to create a breeze – not waved to and fro.

Saurashtra and **Kathiwar** make fixed fans, crescent or axe-shaped with a variety of wooden handles. The leaf of the fan is hard cardboard covered with colored cloth, embellished with colored glass beads sewn into designs: Peacocks, Parrots, Elephants, Horses, human figures, etc. The edges have small rounds of velvet or cloth beads hanging an inch or more from the edge.

Punjab: In this region a wedding fan was usually made and given to the bride by her parents as part of her household effects. Sometimes it was made by the bride herself. It is usually in the halberd shape attached to a wooden handle. The material has brightly colored appliqués and is trimmed with lace and ribbon. In another part of Punjab, a sister has to fan her brother before he leaves for his wedding; he then rewards her with some payment.

Madhya Pradesh (central provinces): A *Fixed Wooden Fan*, squarish with a round, light wooden stick handle is made here. The leaf consists of interwoven wooden sticks. In the center, various designs such as two lovers, landscapes, birds, human or mythological figures are printed.

Bihar, Assam, Tripura (and other North Eastern states): These states make *Winnowing Fans* for threshed rice or millet. The *Rengma Nagas* of Assam believe that anyone who destroys a *Winnowing Fan* will die. Other types from these states are: *Cockades* made of Cane, opening to a complete circle with handles made of Bamboo; *Brisés* made of Cane, dyed or painted red or brown and a 2-piece semi-circular *Folding Fan* where the stick works as a handle with 2 elastic loops to hold the fan open.

Himachal Pradesh (northern): This region makes *Fixed Fans*, oval-shaped on a steel frame, embroidered in navy blue or red with white lace around the edges. The central embroidery is typically a girl holding a fan. The handle is a wooden stick covered with pink or light blue cloth. Another type is an axe-shaped *Leather Fan* with appliqué decoration and a colorful embroidered edging. The handle is turned and painted wood.

Madras: A woven *Fixed Fan* of straw in natural shades or green, dark blue or maroon with the edge stitched with black or red cloth on a wooden stick is made here. Most of the fans have different colored straw and designs on either side. They are used for cooking fires and for personal cooling.

Orissa (a large part of East India, along with West Bengal, Bihar, etc.): In Pipli, a small village famed for production of umbrellas as well as appliqué work, *Flag Fans* are made. Typically they are round cloth fans fixed to the side of their handles. The leaf is made in various colors with appliqué motifs such as flowers, birds and animals with small circular or square mirrors embedded in four or five places between the appliqué. The wooden handle is covered with cloth and on the bottom is a small wooden cylinder about 5 inches in length where the fan is held and twirled. Large *Temple Fans* (up to 5 feet) are also made here.

Tamil Nadu (southernmost part of India): In **Rameswaran**, a place of pilgrimage, fans are made for souvenirs. These are *Cockades* made of Palm leaves, secured with string, with sticks of Palm wood.

Uttar Pradesh (northern): Varanasi or Benares make *Temple Fans* in small, medium and large sizes ranging from 5–12 inches, including the handle. These come in pairs and are made of silk brocade, metallic fabrics or velvet. On some, small, round or square-cut mirrors are embedded in the velvet or brocade. These fans can also be found outside big temples in Mumbai and other major cities.

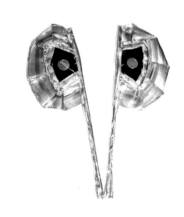

Rajasthan: Round *Fixed Fans*, about 9 inches in diameter are made of Khus, Vetiver, Cucus or Ver Root, all materials that can be sprinkled with water before fanning for an extra cooling effect. Cloth hangings are tied onto three sides of Ver Root fans. As with similarly shaped *Fixed Fans*, the wooden handle is whirled to create a breeze. Round, *Fixed Fans* of Khus, with edges covered with white or red cloth, are used in temples, kept behind the deity and used mainly in the summer. Round *Fixed Fans* covered with attractive Peacock feathers are popular with tourists. These vary in size from 12 inches to almost three feet.

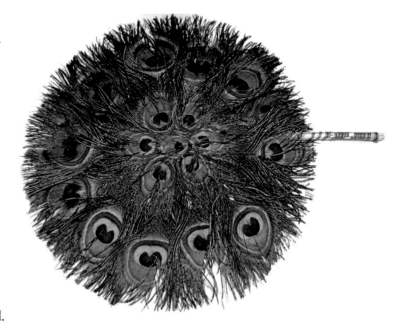

BURMA: In Burma, northwest India and **Assam**, *Winnowing Fans* are used for threshed grain. One person pours the grain (usually rice or millet) from a height while another fans it with the *Winnowing Fan* to blow the chaff away before the grain reaches the ground.

Buddhist monks have used fans as a symbol of religious authority for many centuries. Typical of those made today are roundish-ovals, 15" wide x 14" long with a 6" plastic handle. The leaf may be a simple Palm leaf, varnished and bound around the edge with dark red corduroy or a double layer of dark red corduroy over a frame, ornamented with the 24 *Patthana sutras* (holy verses) painted in off-white. These fans are large enough to protect a monk's bald head from the sun and can be set on a stand to block his view and prevent distractions while he chants the *sutras*.

SRI LANKA: A common type is a *Screen Fan* woven of natural and dyed straw with the handle covered with plain woven straw.

Far from an exhaustive list of *Ethnographic Fans*, these brief sketches are compiled from the writings of individuals living in or familiar with these areas who have documented local fan making and use, providing evidence that even in this fast-paced, high-tech world, there are many places where fans are not only still being made, but remain a vital part of the local culture.

Access to Fans

Fans in Museums

The five fan museums are important in introducing fans to the public. General museums and historical societies with fan collections occasionally bring fans out of storage for exhibits and would probably do so more often, if asked. Due to their age and delicate nature, fans are ideally kept in storage under temperature-controlled conditions and away from the light. Because of this, museums that can afford to do so are photographing their fans and making the images available on their websites.

Viewing Fans and Learning More About Them

Since the last quarter of the 20thC, many hand fan books have been published. For electronic access, hand fan sites on the internet reach a world-wide audience. Good images are the next best thing to holding a fan in your hand and become even more interesting when accompanied by descriptive text. Be sure to specify <u>hand</u> fans in your search. These sites are often privately set up and maintained by *fanistas*, many of whom are members of fan organizations. Larger fan organizations also have their own websites.

Purchasing Fans

If you are traveling abroad, especially in those countries that still make fans, you can usually come home with some interesting fans. If you're not leaving home, the internet's auction sites make buying easy. Electronic auctions have largely replaced live auctions in the U.S., though live auctions with fans are still held in Europe. The internet has also made it easy to purchase a wide variety of *Advertising*, *Souvenir* or *Commemorative Fans*, customized to your needs. Most of those come from Spain or the Orient. In larger U.S. cities that have Chinatowns or Japantowns, fans are available in souvenir shops. Museum gift shops, especially in the South, often carry fans - both as souvenirs and to make strolling around more comfortable. Hand fans can sometimes be found in antique or second-hand shops and though this is increasingly rare, it never hurts to ask.

Finally, for access to fans, don't overlook fan organizations. They offer resources and provide opportunities to see and acquire fans. The larger organizations publish illustrated articles on a wide variety of fan-related topics and the festive get-togethers of these groups are frequently marked with a *Commemorative Fan*, often designed by a club member.

GLOSSARY

A l'Anglaise: Ribs of the fan applied to a single leaf and visible on the reverse, sometimes painted over.

Articulated Fan: A fan with moving part(s). In a *Folding Fan*, the articulated part is usually enclosed in an oval on the guard and activated by a thin rod located beneath or alongside it.

Assignat Fan: A *Printed Fan* made during the French Revolution, covered with trompe l'oeil *assignats*, a form of paper money issued from 1789-1796 by the National Assembly. *Assignats* became essentially worthless, causing hyperinflation and adding to France's woes during this period.

Atelier: French for workshop, esp. that of an artist in fine or decorative arts where a principal master works with assistants, apprentices and students to produce pieces released under the master's name.

Battoir sticks: Ornate fan blades, traditionally in the shape of flattened guitars or racquets; these were large and few in number, typically six – eight. Other large, and unusually shaped blades are also commonly referred to as *battoir*.

Blades: The sticks of a *Brisé Fan* and the sticks below the leaf on a *Pleated Fan* which are typically wider than the sticks supporting the leaf.

Brisé: (*Brisé* - from the French "broken.") A leafless, folding fan made of overlapping blades, held at the base by a rivet and at the top by a string or ribbon near the upper edge.

Cabriolet: A pleated fan with two (and occasionally) three leaves mounted so that a portion of the widely spaced sticks is visible between the leaves.

Cartouche: See Medallion.

Celluloid: A highly flammable early plastic made from a mixture of camphor and cellulose nitrate. *Celluloid* could be tinted any color, marbleized, pearlized or made to simulate tortoiseshell, ivory or horn. It was made between about 1860 and 1950 when it was replaced by newer plastics.

Chasing: A decorative technique used on metal where the design is created by hammering into the material. See *Repoussé*.

Chatelaine: A decorative belt hook or clasp worn at the waist from which were suspended chains. Each chain held a small object a woman wished to keep handy, e.g, keys, watch, scissors, fan, etc.

Chinoiserie: *Chinoiserie* is a Westernized take on elements of Chinese, Japanese, Persian and Indian decoration (and sometimes a combination of styles). The West's love affair with exotic "Oriental Style" decoration which meant anything coming from east of Constantinople began shortly after the *Age of Exploration* brought arts of the East to Europe. *Chinoiserie* was at its height in the the late 1600's through the third quarter of the 18thC. The term itself was not coined till the 19thC.

Cloisonné: On metal mesh or filigree fans, this is decorative enamel work. Designs are created by soldering on cells (*cloisons*) which contain the colored, fired and glazed pigment. China is known for excelling at this type of work.

Clouté: Applied or inset tablets of mother-of-pearl or other decorative materials, pinned with metal thread.

Cockade: A fan with a pleated or brisé leaf that opens from 180 to 360 degrees around its handle(s) because the pivot is at the center instead of the base. Some *Cockades* can be retracted into an open-ended case/handle. Large novelty *Cockades*, made with an angle adjustment, can double as small parasols. The *Cockade* was a popular type for 20thC *Advertising Fans*.

Decoupé: Elaborate patterns in skin or paper cut with tiny scissors, pricked with pins or stamped out. (Think of machine-cut paper lace doilies.) Early European *Decoupé Fans* resemble the geometric patterns of reticella lace.

Duck Foot Fan: One of the earliest (16thC) *Pleated Fans* used by the ladies of Ferrara, Italy. It got its name because when fully opened to a quarter circle, it resembled the webs between a duck's toes. It was mounted on 8 very narrow ivory sticks. The leaves were formed of strips of vellum, often inset with mica, delicately painted and topped with ball finials.

Fan: In other languages: Latin: *vannus* (the English *fan* comes from this root word); French: *éventail*; Spanish: *abanico*; Portuguese: *abano*; Dutch: *waaier*; German: *fächer*; Italian: *ventaglio*; Polish: *wachlarz*; Japanese: *ogi* (*Folding Fan*); *uchiwa* (*Screen Fan*). The Japanese add dozens of other modifers to *ogi* and *uchiwa* to describe specific types; Chinese: *pien-mien* (*Screen Fan*); *che shan* (*Folding Fan*); *hu shan* (*Brisé Fan*) and *t'uan shan* (round *Pole Fan* used at important occasions and in processions); Korean: *dandeon* (round *Screen Fan*) and *hapjukseon* (*Folding Fan*); India: *pankhā*.

Fanista: Any individual - whether formally affiliated with fans or not - who finds him/herself besotted with fans.

Fête Champêtre: French for a countryside outing or picnic. Influenced by the work of *Rococo* artists, this was a popular subject on 18thC fans. Aristocrats were often portrayed dressed as shepherds and shepherdesses, frolicking in idealized pastoral settings.

Filigree: Delicate tracery ornamentation of gold, silver or copper wire.

Fire Screen: A type of *Fixed Fan* whose primary purpose was to protect the holder from the heat of a fireplace. They had fairly long handles (8"-10") were usually made in pairs, often were highly ornamented and when not in use adorned the mantel of the fireplace.

Fixed Fan: Also called a *Screen Fan*. A rigid fan that does not fold. Many variations exist.

Flag Fan: This early type is made of stiff or flexible material, side-mounted to a thin handle so that it resembles a flag on a flagpole. Unlike other fans made to be waved to and fro, if you are fanning yourself with a *Flag Fan*, twirl it around in a circle to create a breeze.

Fontange: A fan shape named for an 18thC hairstyle. The guards are shorter than the leaf at its highest point which produces a pointed, arched shape when open. Similar fans, with guards shorter than the apex of the fan, though more rounded in shape than the *Fontange* are the *Forme Ballon* (fan shaped like a hot air balloon) and the *Shell-Shaped Fan*, resembling a scallop shell. All three were popular in the early 20thC.

Folding Fan: A fan that closes on itself. The primary types are: *Pleated, Brisés* and *Cockades. Cockades* may be either pleated or brisé.

Fly Whisk: A fan of great antiquity. It consists of a handle to which are attached grasses or other plant materials, long feathers, e.g., Ostrich or Peacock or the tails of animals such as Elephants, Horses, Deer And Yaks. In many cultures *Fly Whisks* have been/are symbols of authority.

Fretting/Fret Work: An interlaced decorative design either carved in low relief on a solid background or cut out with a special saw(s). Most fretwork patterns are geometric in design.

Gorge: The area on the blades and guard immediately above the head. On a *Brisé* the gorge may be defined by painted or carved decoration or by shaping of the closed fan's profile to create a distinct area.

Gouache: An opaque water paint, lightened with white and traditionally thickened with gum and honey. Because of its special properties, gouache is commonly used on fan leaves. It has the advantages of being an elastic medium, provides a firm body, does not crack and its light tones are delicate and velvety.

Guards: Also called guardsticks. The outer sticks that protect folding fans. They are usually heavier, stronger and extend the full length of the fan to give added strength when in use and to protect the leaf or blades when closed. Guards are often more highly decorated than other sticks.

Head: A counter-intuitive term because it refers to the lower end of a fan where the rivet is located.

Hiramakie: Japanese: "flat sprinkled picture." A lacquer technique where gold or silver powder is used to form designs by sprinkling it onto a lacquer ground before it has hardened. These leave slightly raised areas and the whole area is then covered with clear lacquer. See *Takamakie*.

Horn: A natural plastic obtained from horns, hooves and nails of various animals, made malleable with heat, then pressed or cast.

Intarsia: Stone or marble decoration where the material used to form patterns and designs is cut and inlaid into a hard surface ground. Unlike mosaic, the ground does not show through in *intarsia*.

Japanning: The European process developed as a substitute for Oriental lacquer, tradionally using varnish, shellac and spirits of wine.

Japonisme: The great enthusiasm for Japan and Japanese art in the West beginning in the last quarter of the 19thC, when Japan opened its ports. Japanese art, seen for the first time in centuries, had a large influence on the arts, crafts and design of the West.

Jenny Lind Fan: See *Palmette*

Leaf: The pleated arc of silk, paper or skin placed over the sticks on a single leaf *Pleated Fan*. If a double leaf, the sticks are secured between two layers of material.

Lithography: A printing process possible because of the natural repulsion of oil and water. A design is drawn in reverse on (traditionally) a limestone surface with a crayon or ink containing grease. The stone is then treated with acid and gum arabic which etches the portion of the stone not protected by the grease-based image. When water is applied to the stone, the etched areas retain moisture. The stone is inked with a roller which adheres to the oil-treated area. Finally, the ink is transferred to a blank piece of paper using a flat print plate thus producing a printed page. This new form of printing was much faster, allowed for much longer runs, was less expensive and rendered a wider range of tones and effects than earlier printing methods. Lithography was invented in 1796 by *Alois Senefelder*, followed in 1837 by *Godefroy Engelmann's* process, chromolithography, that added color. By the middle to the end of the 19thC these two printing innovations had become very important to the printing of fans.

Loop: A small half-round or U-shaped attachment to the head of the fan, held in place by the rivet. They were commonly made of metal, ivory or tortoiseshell. With a loop, a fan may be suspended from a cord or ribbon and worn on the wrist – or attached to a chatelaine. Loops were uncommon before the mid-19thC but were sometimes added later to an earlier fan.

Marquetry: A form of veneer work in which small, thin pieces of wood, bone, ivory, mother-of-pearl, tortoiseshell, straw, brass or other metals are cut and applied to a solid ground to form designs, patterns and pictures.

Medallion: A framed oval or round, usually enclosing a portrait, monogram or small scene. Although a *cartouche* has an elongated, rectangular shape with rounded corners (think Egyptian *cartouches*), the terms *cartouche* and medallion are often used interchangeably in fan descriptions.

Mica: Thin sheets of various minerals found in igneous rocks. Mica splits in one direction only, enabling it to be split into very thin, almost transparent sheets which are, despite their delicate appearance, quite strong. Mica scales, cut into small panels are sometimes used to adorn fans.

Monture: The "skeleton" or hard frame of a *Pleated Fan*, comprised of the sticks, guards and rivet.

Motif: A distinctive theme, subject or feature, often repeated.

Mount: Another term for the fan's leaf (not to be confused with the monture).

Obverse: The front of the fan; the side facing the viewer. "Recto" is also commonly used for the front.

Ogi: Japanese *Folding Fans*. Because of the historical and continuing importance of fans in Japanese culture, there are many types of Ogi, each made for a specific purpose and with a specific name. For example, the *Akome Ogi* is a *Brisé* associated only with the court. It is made of 25-39 Cypress wood sticks, painted with white lead, decorated with gold and silver leaf and painted with flowers. Long, multi-colored cords, trailing to the ground, hang from the guards. The *Rikyu Ogi*, or tea ceremony fan, is an *Ogi* with few (usually 3) sticks and a simple leaf. It is used in the tea ceremony to pass small cakes (not for fanning). The *Gunsen* was a folding war fan introduced perhaps as early as the 11thC. This *Ogi* was made of 10-12 iron or lacquered wood sticks, very thick double leaves and guards of brass or iron. One side would be painted with the moon and the other with the sun. This fan was used by generals, *samurai*, court nobles and officers. During times of peace, the *Gunsen* was carried on ceremonial occasions by men in full armor. Still another type is the *Mai Ogi*, a dance fan. They have about 10 Bamboo sticks and a leaf of paper, silk or satin, painted with decorations appropriate to the occasion. The guards are attached by cords for balance. The rivet secures a small piece of lead countersunk in both guards which, by adding weight to the fan's base, permits more graceful movements. *Mai Ogi* are used by dancers, including actors in *Kabuki* and *Noh* theater. These four *Ogi* represent just a few of the many varieties.

Palmette: A *Palmette Fan* is a *Brisé* with paper, fabric or ocassionally leather blades made in the shape of a leaf, flower petal or feather. Fans of this kind are also commonly called *Jenny Lind Fans*.

Panniers: A hoop skirt fashion made with a frame that created an exaggerated extension on either side of a woman's hips.

Pastiche: On a fan, a painted scene in the style of a different period. 19thC fan makers made many pastiche fans, copying the styles of 18thC and earlier fans.

Piqué: Decoration of gold, silver or steel dots inlaid into sticks and guards. The stick is pierced with a tiny drill and the minute dots are inserted flush with the surface.

Putti: Plural of *putto*, a small cherub. *Putti* are a frequent decorative element on 18th and 19th century fans having romantic or classical themes. Though the *putto* is said to be wingless, most cherubs on fans do have wings, but are commonly called "*putti.*" To distinguish Cupid who always has wings, he is usually depicted with bow, arrow and quiver, sometimes blindfolded to indicate the haphazard strike of love.

Repoussé: A decorative metalworking technique where the material is hammered on the reverse side to create a raised design on the front – the opposite of chasing. The two techniques are often used on the same piece for maximum effect.

Reserves: Spaces in the outer part of the fan leaf containing decoration subordinate to the main picture.

Reticella: A needle lace dating from the 15thC. This was originally a form of cutwork in which threads were pulled from linen to make a grid on which the pattern was stitched using a buttonhole stitch. Later *reticella* used a grid of thread; both methods resulted in a characteristic geometric design of squares and circles with arched or scalloped borders.

Reticule: An early drawstring handbag.

Ribs: Upper part of the fan sticks that support the leaf. These are not seen if the fan has a double leaf or if the leaf is made of opaque material. Ribs are often thinner than the lower (visible) blades and are sometimes made of a different material.

Rivet: A pin running through the head of the sticks, allowing the sticks to open and close while holding them together. Rivets may be held in place with plain button heads on either end of the pin or be capped with decorative "washers" made of mother-of-pearl, paste or even real jewels.

Russian Leather: A leather originally from Russia, but subsequently made elsewhere in Europe. The characteristic color, a russet/oxblood red, was obtained by blending red Sandalwood, Brazilian wood and limewater. A pleasant odor came from soaking the leather with oil distilled from Birch bark. Many Russian leather brisé fans or Russian leather-covered sticks and guards were made in Austria after 1869.

Screen Fan: See *Fixed Fan.*

Sequins: Sparkly round decorations, originally made of metal.

Shibayama: A Japanese family of craftsmen, established in the 18thC who specialized in the decoration of *inro* (small containers of interlocking wooden sections, decorated, lacquered and worn suspended from the sash of a kimono). On fans this work is characterized by minute pieces of inlay that stand in relief. Guards with flower and insect motifs are frequently seen on *Shibayama*-style work.

Shoulder: The uppermost part of the blades where they meet the leaf. In most cases blades will be straight across or rounded. Shoulders may be either prominent and wide or not well defined.

Skin: A term used to designate an animal source for the leaf of a fan or the covering of a fan's blades or guards - without specifying parchment, vellum, kid, etc. Precise identification is a tricky business, best left to the experts.

Spangles: Sparkly decorations, made in a great variety of shapes – other than round. See *Sequins.*

Squelette (A la Squelette): Fan blades, usually quite thin and spaced wide apart.

Takamakie: Japanese: "high sprinkled picture." Similar to *hiramakie*, but design areas are raised by adding charcoal or grinding powder and raw lacquer before the sprinkled metal powders. See *Hiramakie.*

Tortoiseshell: There are 3 types of animals that live in a rigid, bony shell, comprised of a top and bottom half: 1) the tortoise who lives on dry land; 2) the terrapin that usually inhabits rivers and lakes and 3) marine turtles who spend their lives cruising the world's tropical and temperate oceans, coming ashore only to excavate nests and lay their eggs. "Tortoise" was the name given to all these creatures hundreds of years ago and the name tortoiseshell stuck, though "turtleshell" would be more accurate when describing the material once used in fans. Only Green and Hawksbill Turtles have a carapace (upper shell) thick/durable enough to be useful as a craftable material. Fan sticks and blades come almost exclusively from the Hawksbill Turtle.

Trompe l'oeil: French for "Fool the eye." A flat surface painted to look like a real object.

Uchiwa: A large category of Japanese *Fixed Fans*, each with a distinct name. For example, the *Gumpai-uchiwa*, a battle fan, was made of iron, heavily lacquered wood or hardened leather and used by a commander to signal a surge or retreat in battle. This fan was typically decorated with the sun, moon and stars. Today a similar fan, the *Gyoji-uchiwa*, a smaller version, is used by referees in *Sumo* wrestling matches. The *Maki-uchiwa* is a compact Bamboo fan with a circular mount that can be inserted into a slot in the handle for fanning and then rolled around the handle and secured with a thread or cord when not in use. The *Mizu-uchiwa*, a water fan, is made of Bamboo split into segments and covered with sturdy paper. The fan is dipped in oil and persimmon juice to make it impermeable to water and when dry, it's lightly sealed with varnish. The user dips the fan into water, thus gaining the cooling advantage of evaporating water while fanning. The *Yamato-uchiwa* is a surprise fan. Two sheets of very fine silk, gauze or semi-transparent paper are stretched over a rigid frame and some object, e.g., a flower or butterfly is slipped between the two sheets. The fan looks quite plain till held up to the light which reveals the treasure inside. These are just a few examples of the many types of *Uchiwa*.

Vernis Martin: A name commonly used to describe *Brisé Fans* with the entire surface elaborately painted with oils and then coated with clear varnish for a lustrous finish. They are named for the 18thC Martin family of France, famous makers of varnished ware – though there is no record that the Martins ever made any fans.

Verso: Reverse side of the fan – the side facing the user while the public sees the obverse.

Vignette: A small illustration, usually not the primary design.

Washers: Small, usually circular caps placed over both ends of the rivet. These were frequently made of mother-of-pearl.

BIBLIOGRAPHY – Books/Catalogs

Alexander, Helene. ALEXANDRE: FAN-MAKER TO THE COURTS OF EUROPE. (Exhibition of Alexandre Fans at the Fan Museum, Sept. 2011, Greenwich). London: The Fan Museum, 2012.

_____. FANS. (The Costume Accessories Series). Great Britain: B.T. Batsford, Ltd., 1984.

Armstrong, Nancy. THE BOOK OF FANS. Surrey: Colour Library International, Ltd., 1978.

_____. A COLLECTOR'S HISTORY OF FANS. New York: Clarkson N. Potter, Inc., 1974.

_____. FANS. London: Souvenir Press, Ltd., 1984.

_____. FANS IN SPAIN. London: Philip Wilson Publishers, 2004.

Bennett, Anna G. & Berson, Ruth. FANS IN FASHION. (Exhibition at the Fine Arts Museum of San Francisco, California Palace of the Legion of Honor, May 23-August 30, 1981). Vermont: Charles E., Tuttle Co., Inc., 1981.

Bennett, Anna Gray. UNFOLDING BEAUTY – THE ART OF THE FAN: THE COLLECTION OF ESTHER OLDHAM & THE MUSEUM OF FINE ARTS, BOSTON. (Exhibition March 9-June 5, 1988.), Boston: Museum of Fine Arts, 1988.

Blum, Dilys. FANS FROM THE COLLECTION. Published in *The Bulletin*, Vol. 84, Nos. 358, 359., Philadelphia: Philadelphia Museum of Art, 1988.

de Vere Green, Bertha. A COLLECTOR'S GUIDE TO FANS OVER THE AGES. London: Frederick Muller, 1975.

Debrett's Peerage. FANS FROM THE EAST. London: Debrett's Peerage Ltd. in association with The Fan Circle and The Victoria & Albert Museum, 1978.

Fan Circle International. ROYAL FANS. (Exhibition of Fans owned by British Royalty at the Harewood House, Yorkshire, March 26-June 22 and July 7-September 29, 1986). Perth: 1986.

The Fan Museum. COLLECTORS' CHOICE. (Exhibition May 16 - October 1, 1995). London: 1995.

_____. ROYAL FANS: AN EXHIBITION TO COMMEMORATE THE GOLDEN JUBILEE. (Exhibition of British Royal Fans to Commemorate the 50th year of Queen Elizabeth II's reign, 2002). London: 2002.

Fendel, Cynthia. CELLULOID HAND FANS. Dallas: Hand Fan Productions, 2001.

_____. NOVELTY HAND FANS: FASHIONABLE, FUNCTIONAL, FUN ACCESSORIES OF THE PAST. Dallas: Hand Fan Productions, 2006.

Gostelow, Mary. THE FAN. Dublin: Gill & Macmillan Ltd., 1976.

Hart, Avril and Taylor, Emma. FANS. New York: Quite Specific Media Group, Ltd., 1998.

Hutt, Julia and Alexander, Helene. OGI: A HISTORY OF THE JAPANESE FAN. London: Dauphin Publishing, Ltd., 1992.

Irons, Neville John. FANS OF IMPERIAL CHINA. Hong Kong: Kaiserreich Kunst, Ltd., 1981.

_____. FANS OF IMPERIAL JAPAN. Hong Kong: Kaiserreich Kunst, Ltd., 1981.

Kao, Mayching (editor). THE CHENG XUN TANG COLLECTION OF PAINTING & CALLIGRAPHY ON FANS. Hong Kong: Art Museum, the Chinese University of Hong Kong, 1996.

Kirby, Mandy. A VICTORIAN FLOWER DICTIONARY: THE LANGUAGE OF FLOWERS COMPANION. New York: Ballantine Books, 2011.

Kraft Bernabei, Corrine, Moradei, Luisa & Tozzi Bellini, Maria Emirena. A WORLD OF PLAITING AND HAND FANS: THE KRAFT & MORADEI COLLECTION. Florence: Edizioni Polistampa, 2008.

Mackay, James. FANS: ORNAMENTS OF LANGUAGE AND FASHION. Edison: Chartwell Books, 2000.

Mayer, Carole E. FANS. (Exhibition at the Vancouver Museum, September 22,1983 - January 8, 1984). Vancouver: The Vancouver Museum, 1983.

Mayor, Susan. COLLECTING FANS. New York: Christie's International Collectors Series. Mayflower Books, 1980.

Mellville, Beryl. THE FAN AND LACE. England: Lochlea Publications, 1991.

Moote, Marjorie. FANS FROM WORLD'S FAIRS AND EXPOSITIONS FROM THE COLLECTION OF MARJORIE MOOTE. Phoenix: Arizona State University New College of Interdisciplinary Arts and Sciences, 2011.

Mourey, Gabriel, Vallance, Aymer, et al. ART NOUVEAU JEWELLERY & FANS. New York: Dover Publications, Inc., 1973.

North, Audrey. AUSTRALIA'S FAN HERITAGE. Brisbane: Boolarong Publications, 1985.

Parmal, Pamela A. BEAUTY IN HAND: THE ART OF THE FAN. (Exhibition of Fans from the Department of Costume & Textiles, Museum of Art, Rhode Island School of Design, June 1-August 18, 1990). Rhode Island: 1990.

Payen-Appenzeller, Pascal. FANCY FANS: THE ART OF COLLECTIBLES. (Fans from the Atelier of Anne Hoguet, Musee de l'eventail, Paris.) Italy, 2001.

Roberts, Jane, Sutcliffe, Prudence & Mayor, Susan. FANS IN THE ROYAL COLLECTION: UNFOLDING PICTURES. London: Royal Collection Enterprises, Ltd., 2005.

Sheridan, Geraldine. LOUDER THAN WORDS: WAYS OF SEEING WOMEN WORKERS IN EIGHTEENTH-CENTURY FRANCE. Lubbock: Texas Tech University Press, 2009.

Steele, Valerie. THE FAN: FASHION AND FEMININITY UNFOLDED. New York: Rizzoli Int'l. Publications, Inc.

Tsang, Ka Bo. MORE THAN KEEPING COOL: CHINESE FANS AND FAN PAINTINGS. (Exhibition of Chinese fans, fan paintings and fan cases in the Royal Ontario Museum and private collections, Nov. 24, 2001 – May 12, 2002.) Toronto: Royal Ontario Museum, 2002.

Unterholzner, Daniela. SOUTHEAST-ASIAN FANS IN HABSBURG COLLECTIONS: EXCHANGE BETWEEN EUROPE AND SOUTHEAST-ASIA IN THE 16TH CENTURY. Lexington, 2010.

van Saanen, Paul & Greenhalgh, Peter. FROM COURT TO CONFECTIONARY. Lausanne: IRL Imprimeries Reunies, 1994.

Volet, Maryse. IMAGINATION & ITS CONTRIBUTION TO FANS: PATENTS DEPOSITED IN FRANCE IN THE 19th CENTURY. Geneva: Presses De L'Imprimerie Medecine et Hygiene, 1988.

_____. PATENTS FOR FANS FILED IN FRANCE DURING THE 20th CENTURY. Geneva: Presses De L'Imprimerie Medecine et Hygiene, 1992.

Walberg, Gretchen. FANS PATENTED IN THE UNITED STATES: A RESEARCH GUIDE TO HAND HELD FANS. Second edition. Published by the author: Sunbury, 1999.

Willcocks, Clive & Yvonne. FANS AND FAN MAKERS: THE CRAFT & HISTORY OF THE WORSHIPFUL COMPANY OF FAN MAKERS. London: The Worshipful Company of Fan Makers, 2000.

TAPES from THE GREAT COURSES produced by The Teaching Company, Chantilly, Virginia: recorded 2002-2013

Alitt, Patrick. VICTORIAN BRITAIN: 36 Lectures.

Armstrong, Dorsey. TURNING POINTS IN MEDIEVAL HISTORY: 24 Lectures.

Benjamin, Craig G. FOUNDATIONS OF EASTERN CIVILIZATION: 48 Lectures.

Bucholz, Robert. LONDON: A SHORT HISTORY OF THE GREATEST CITY IN THE WESTERN WORLD: 24 Lectures.

Daileader, Philip. HOW THE CRUSADES CHANGED HISTORY: 24 Lectures.

Desan, Suzanne M. LIVING THE FRENCH REVOLUTION & THE AGE OF NAPOLEON. 48 Lectures.

Fix, Andrew C. THE RENAISSANCE, THE REFORMATION & THE RISE OF NATIONS: 48 Lectures.

Harl, Kenneth W. ORIGINS OF GREAT ANCIENT CIVILIZATIONS: 12 Lectures.

Kloss, William. A HISTORY OF EUROPEAN ART: 48 Lectures.

JOURNALS Articles appearing in publications of the Fan Association of North America (FANA):

FANA Newsletters:

N.v.2#1   Rhoads, Mary. "Revelations from Tiffany & Co. ca.1910."

N.v.2#2   "Lace on 18thC Costume France."

N.v.2#3   Gershuny, Lenore. "Dress Under Louis XIV (1643-1715)."
Hart, Avril. "The Introduction of the Folding Fan Into Europe."
Rhoads, Mary. "American Fans."

N.v.2#4   Alexander, Helene. "The French Fan."
Gershuny, Lenore. "Costume During the Reign of Louis XV."
Grayson, Grace. "The Ostrich Industry: Farming for Feathers."

N.v.3#1   Gershuny, Lenore. "French Costume 1774-1789."

N.v.4#1   Oldham, Esther. "Vernis Martin Fans."
Rhoads, Mary. "The Empress of China, the China Trade and Philadelphia Fans."

N.v.5#2   "Celluloid."
LACIS. "Lace and Lace Making."
Mayer, Carol E. "Avenues."

N.v.5#3   Moore, Kevin. "Birth of an Industry: Vive la Publicite par L'objet du France."

FANA Quarterlies:

V.6#3   Oldham, Esther. "German Fans."

V.6#4   Bennett, Anna. "Fans as Social History, 1590-1920."
_____. "The Almost Incredible Commerce: the Marketing & Manufacture of Fans."

V.8#2   Johnson, Colin. "A Review of The Opulent Era: Fashions of Worth, Doucet and Pingat."

V.8#3   Cornish, Grace. "Advertising Fans."

V.9#1   "Sally Rand's Famous Fans Turned a Breeze into a Tornado."

V.10#1   Durand-Guedy, Jean Pierre. "Liberated Fans for Liberated Women: Revolutionary Propaganda – Pro & Con."
Johnson, Colin. "Revolution a la Mode: French Costume 1787-1796."

FANA Journals

Fall 2003

DeLeo, Thomas. "The Shell Game."

Moote, Marjorie. "Hair-raising Happenstance: Fontange."

Schiffman, Maurice K. "Japan – the Land of Fans."

Spring 2004

Gould, Sylvie. "A Royalist Fan."

Palmer, Chuck. "A Gift to be Cherished: Plains Indians Modified Peyote Fans."

Ryan, J.P. "Fact and Fiction About Fan Language in the 18th Century."

Fall 2004

Conway, Marguerite. from *Concise Encyclopaedia of Antiques* 1859 "English Fans."

Fall 2005

DeLeo, Thomas. "Tuan Shan: Palace Silk Fans."

Spring 2006

Kowalska, Joanna Regina. "Nineteenth Century Fireside Fans."

Fall 2006

Mazura, Margaretha. "Eros & Amor: Love Iconography on Fans."

Spring 2007

Wagner, Gary. "Tortoiseshell."

Spring 2007

DeLeo, Thomas. "Sequins and Spangles (Paillettes and Paillons)."

Fall 2007

_____ . "Cuir de Russie – Russian Leather."

Spring 2008

Ranftl, David. "The English Fan."

Fall 2008

Mead, George. Excerpt from *A Dictionary of Christian Antiquities*, 1875 "Flabellum."

Spring 2009

Hunt, Edmund Soper. "Excerpt from *Weymouth Ways and Weymouth People: Reminiscences.*"

Fall 2009

Napoli, Giorgio. "From the Commedia del'Arte to Watteau."

Fall 2010

Keith, Margaret. "The Native American Fan."

Spring 2011

DeLeo, Thomas. "All that Glitters is Not Gold: Chinese Export Silver Filigree & Fans."

Fall 2011

Mazura, Margaretha. "Jenny Lind Fans."

Spring 2012

Goettel, Robin. "Fans Enhance Dance Traditions Throughout the World."
Gould, Sylvie. "A North American Bird and Feather Fan."

Fall 2012

Druesedow, Jean L. "Fashion and Fans in Culture and Context."

Spring 2013

Ellerton, Anna. "Mysteries and Secrets Unfold – The Beauty of the Fan."

Fall 2013

McCanless, Christel Ludewig & Wintraecken, Annemiek. "The Art of the Fan in the McFerrin Collection."

Fall 2014

Mazura, Margaretha. "Fantastic Though It's Plastic."

Articles appearing in FANS, the Bulletin of the Fan Circle International (FCI)

#10   Armstrong, Nancy. "Horn Fans."
Oldham, Esther. "The Fascination of Balloons on Fans."

#11   Schneider, Jenny. "Johannes Sulzer: a Winterthur Fan Painter of the Late 18th Century." (continued in #13)

#18   Valabrègue, Anthony. "The Fans of Abraham Bosse."

#19   da Silva, J.B. "Chinese Fans and the Porcelain Trade With the West."

#20   Philippe, Joseph. "A Fan Painted by Marie-Antoinette."
"A Romano-British Fan."

P.S.

Fans are not just for outdoor use in warm weather. Electricity fails and rooms grow stuffy, so always keep a small folding fan in your purse or briefcase. You are sure to stir a conversation along with the breeze!